Contents

Step 2

Unit 7

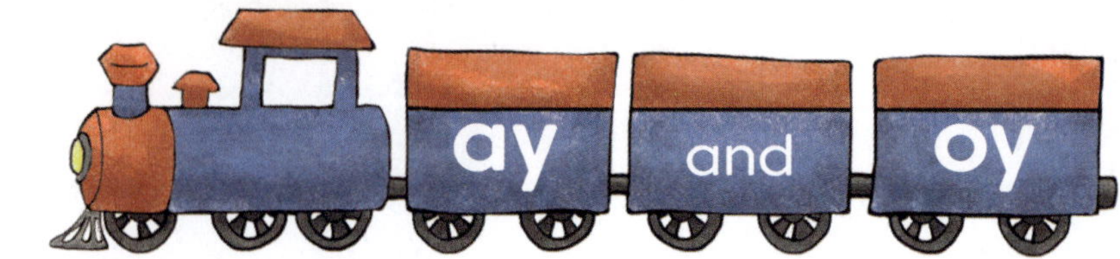

Choose the right spelling of the /ai/ sound for each picture.

tr___

sn___l

r___n

ai ay

h___

spr___

p___nt

Choose the right spelling of the /oi/ sound for each picture.

___l

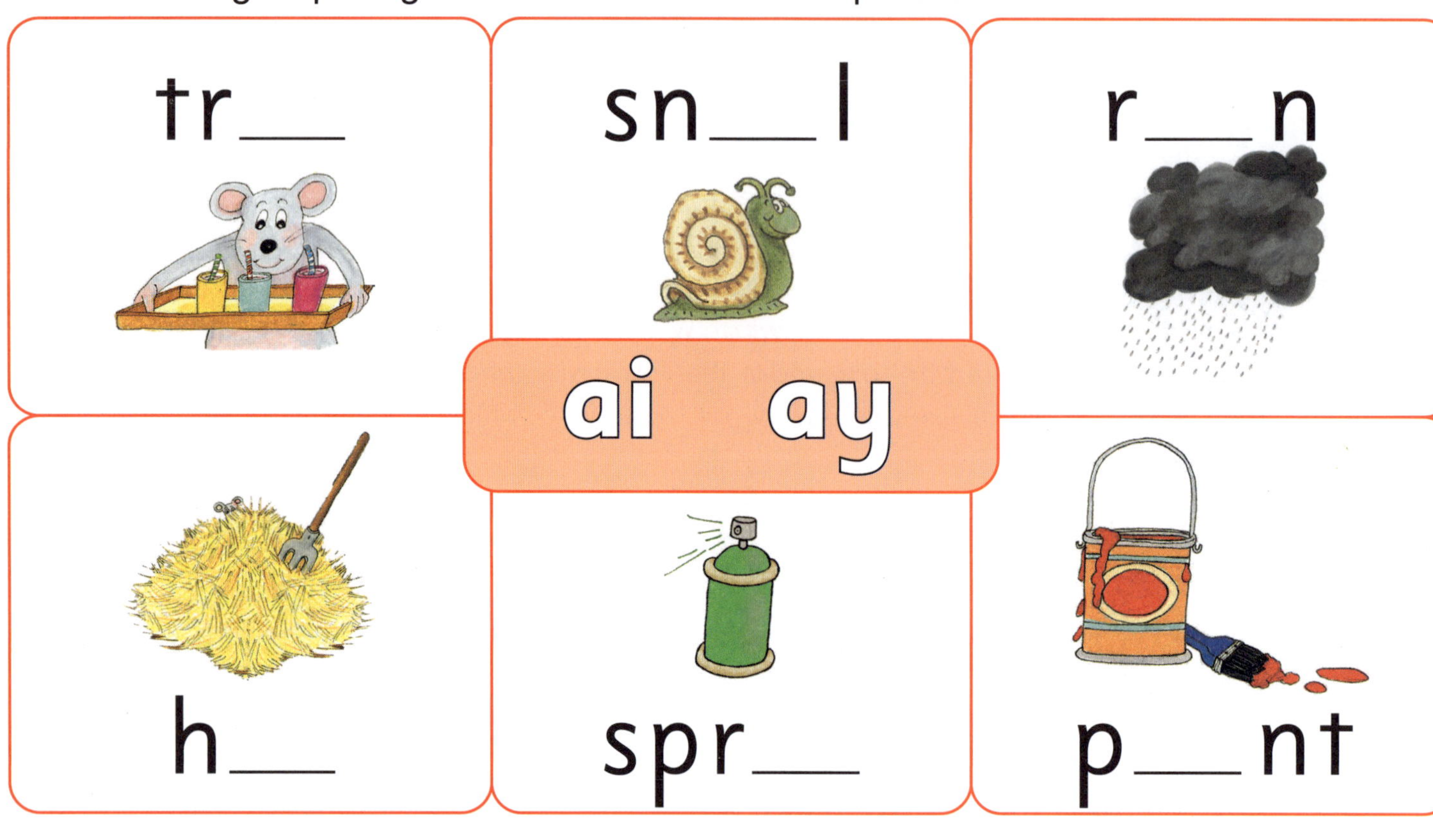

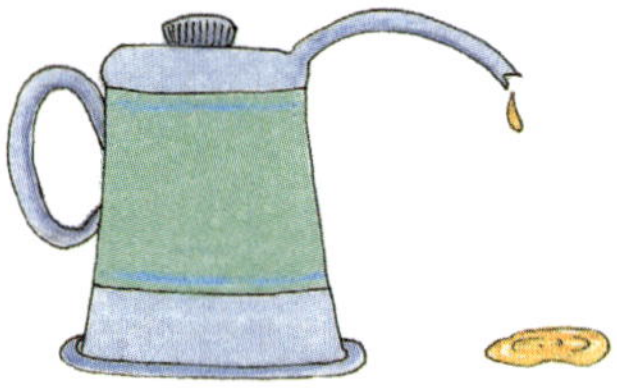

p___nt

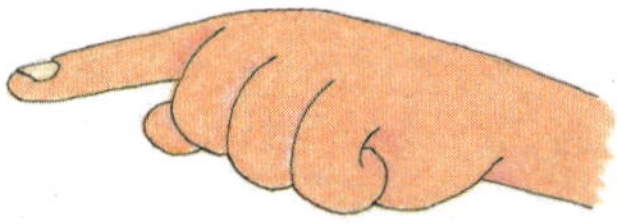

b___

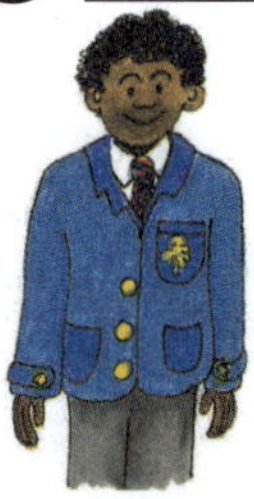

oi oy

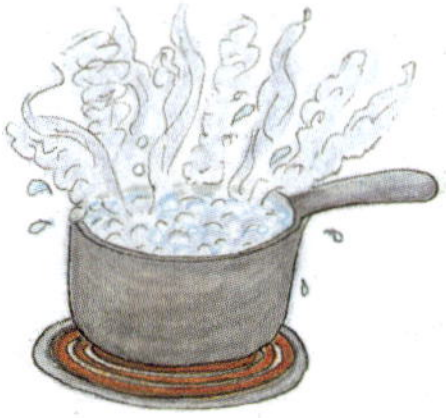

b___l

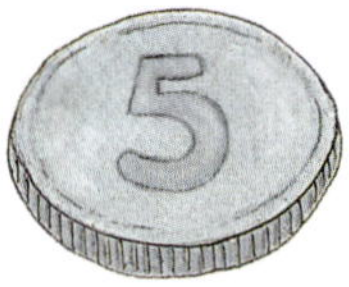

c___n

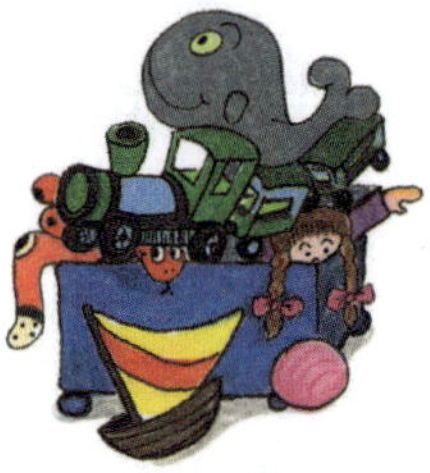

t___box

Handwriting

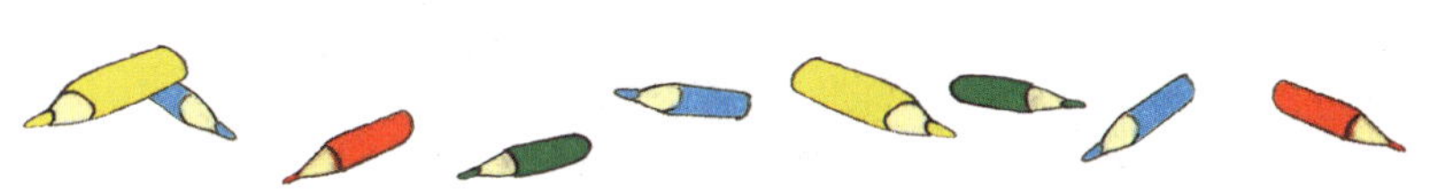

Write the sections of the alphabet in red, yellow, green, or blue.

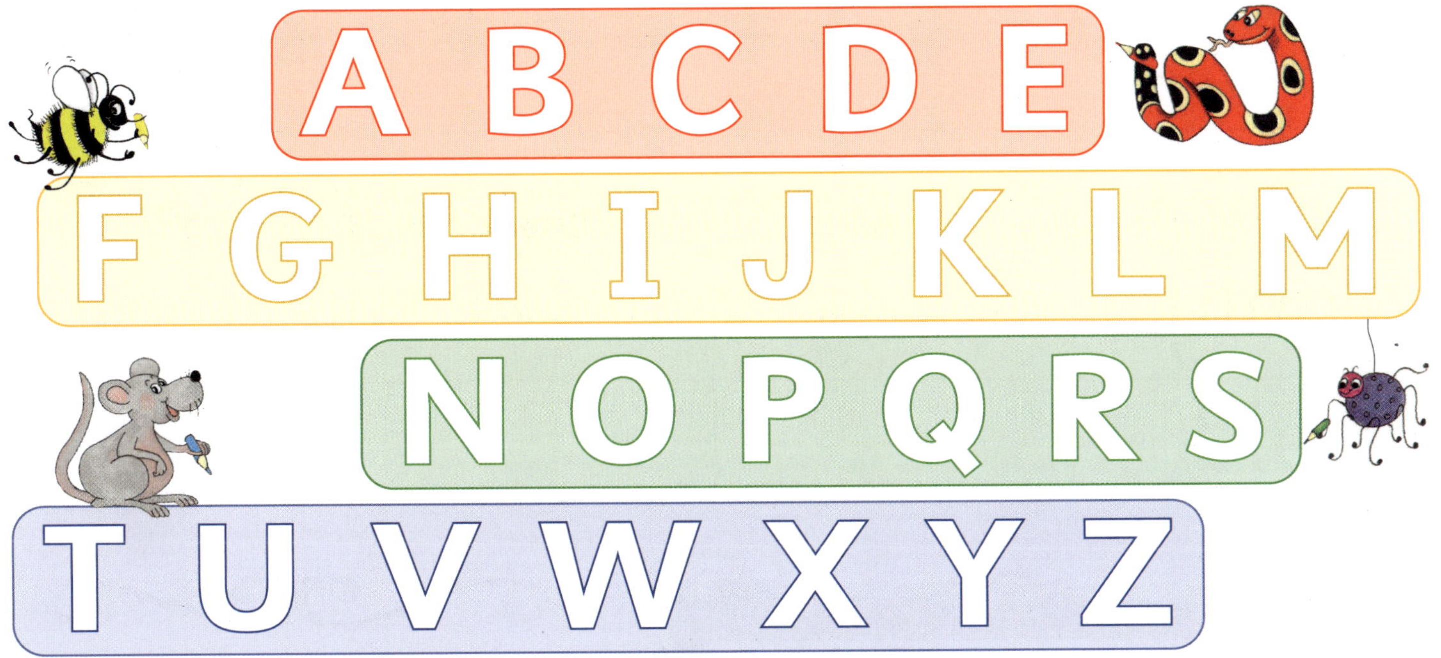

Write the lower-case letter next to each capital letter.

A a B__ C__ D__ E__

F__ G__ H__ I__ J__

K__ L__ M__

Look Find the tricky bit.	**Copy** then **Cover**	**Write** then **Check**	**Have another go!**
only	only		
old	old		

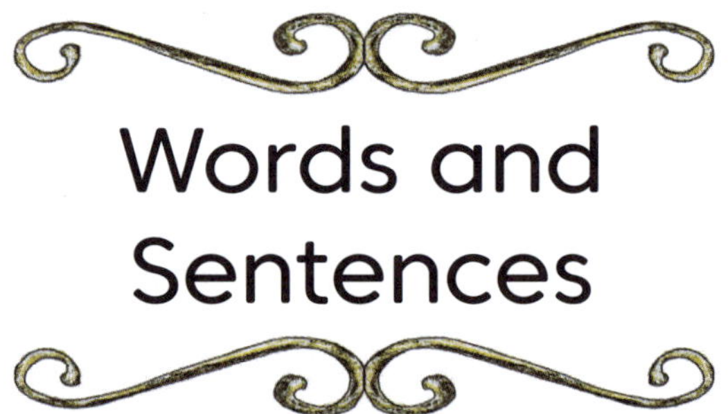

Step 2
Unit 8

As well as ‹ee›, ‹y›, and ‹e_e›, the /ee/ sound can be written as ‹ea›.

seal	teeth	tea
leaf	feet	sheep
tree	read	sea

Read the words at the top of the page and write the correct word under each picture.

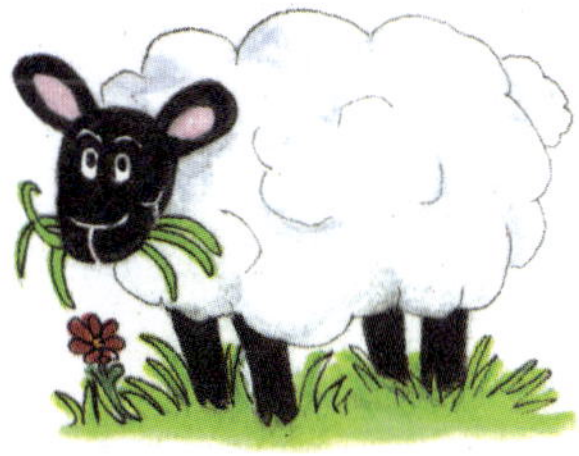

sh ee p	___ ___ ___	___ ___ ___
___ ___	___ ___ ___	___ ___ ___
___ ___ ___	___ ___ ___	___ ___

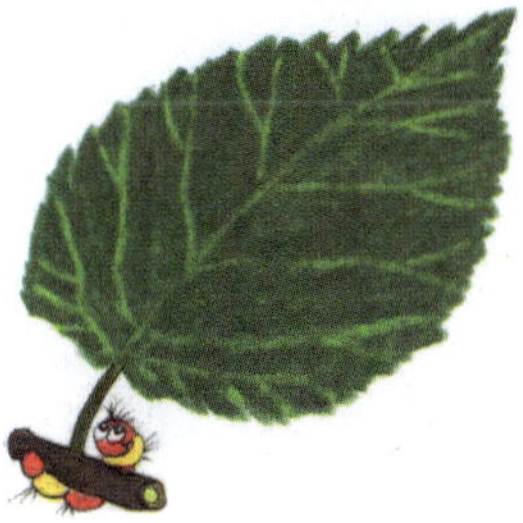

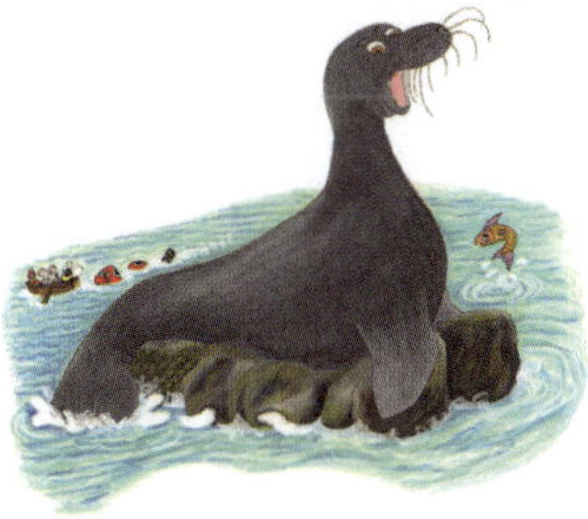

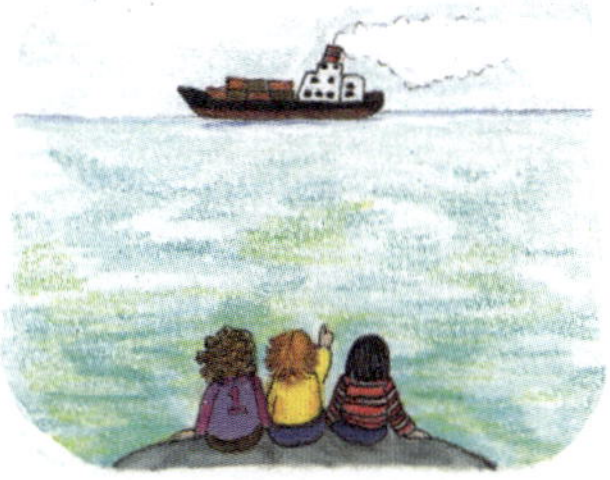

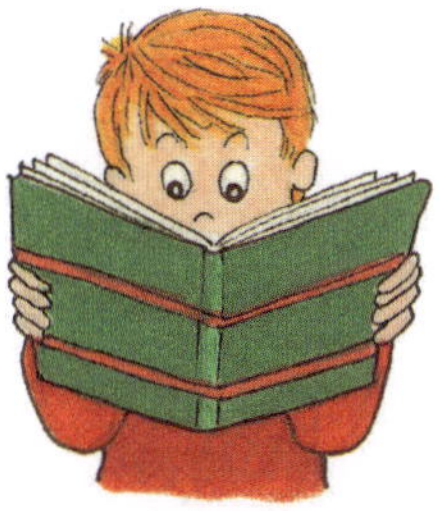

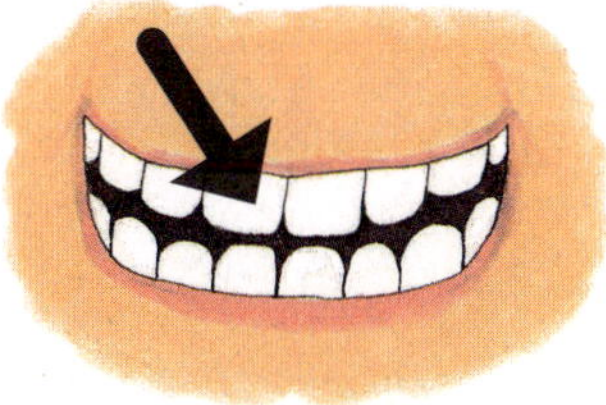

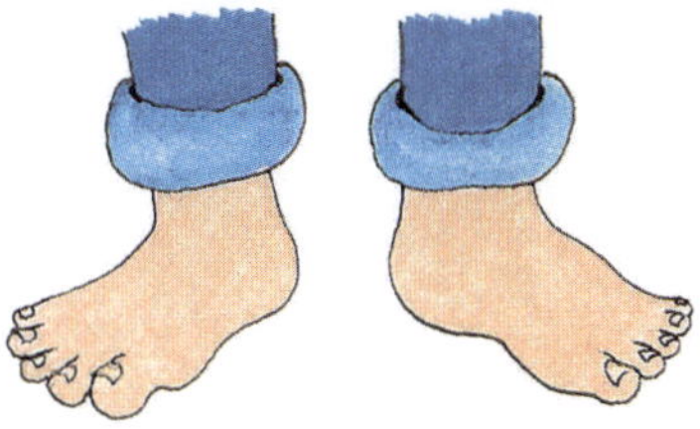

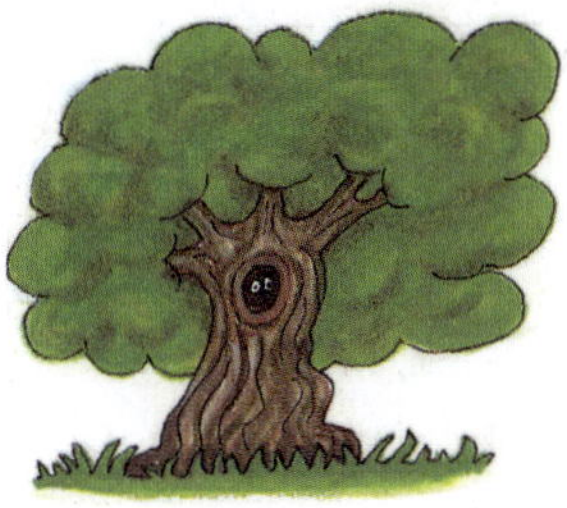

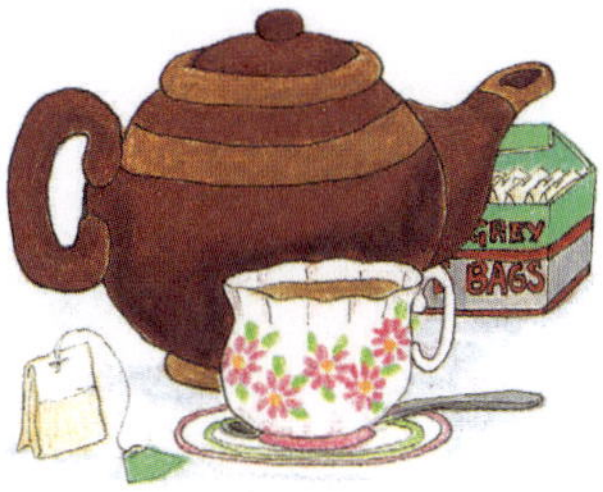

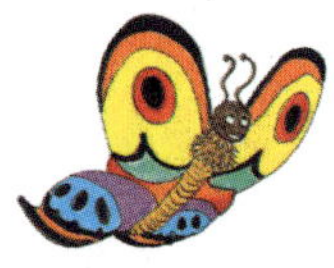

Handwriting

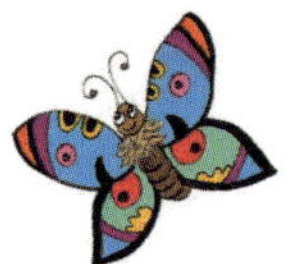

Write over the dotted letters ‹b› and ‹d›.

b b
b b
b b
b b

d d
d d
d d
d d

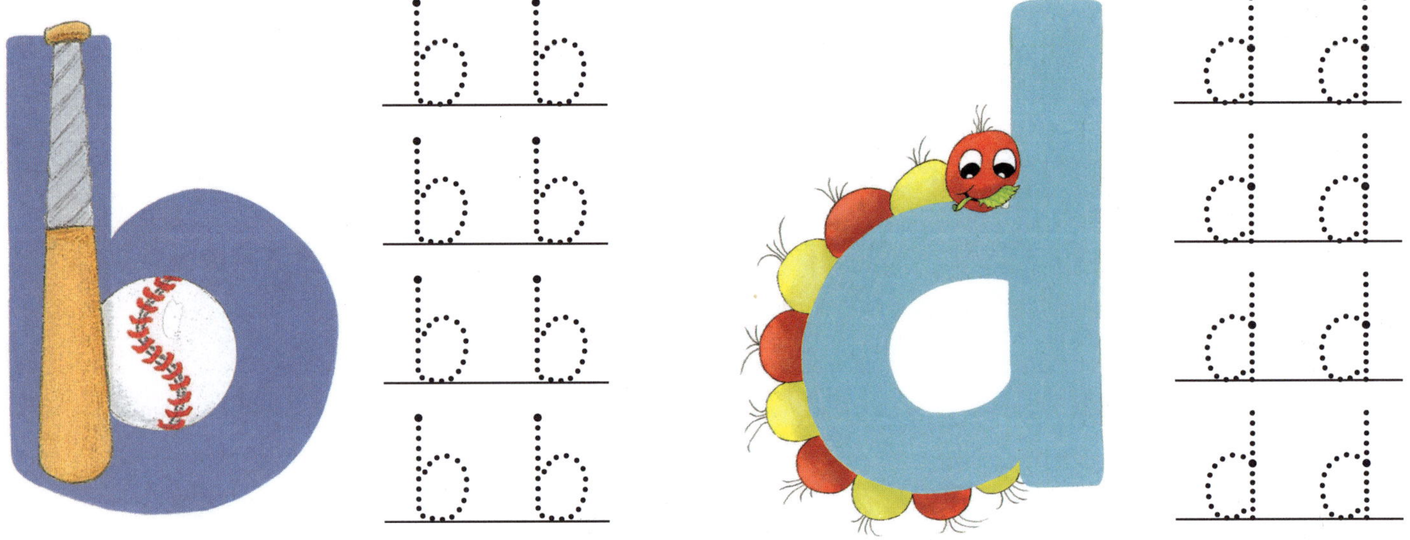

Write the capital letter next to each lower-case letter.

a A

b ___

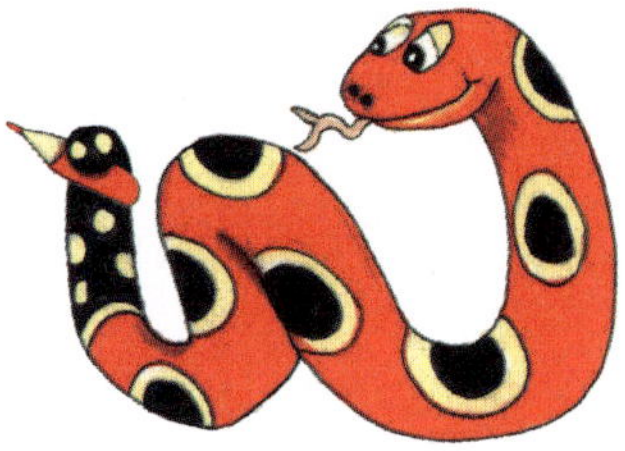

c ___

d ___

e ___

f ___

g ___

h ___

i ___

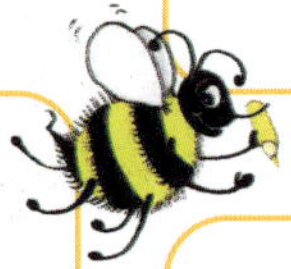

j ___

k ___

l ___

m ___

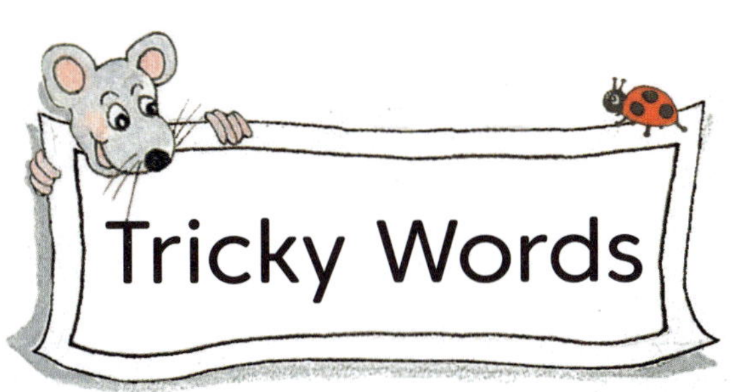

Look Find the tricky bit.	**Copy** then **Cover**	**Write** then **Check**	**Have another go!**
like	like		
have	have		

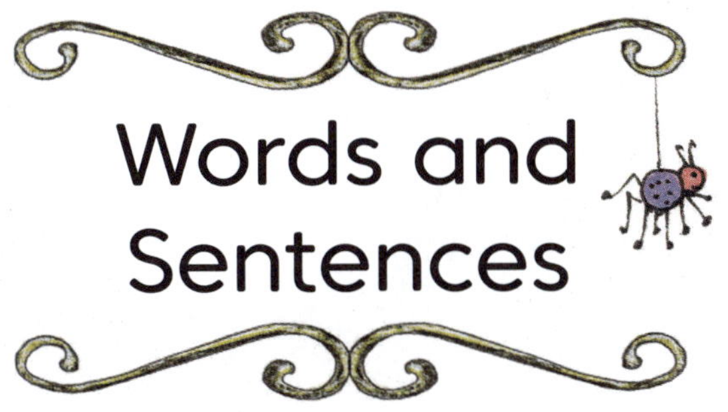

Step 2

Unit 9

y and igh as /ie/

As well as ‹ie› and ‹i_e›, the /ie/ sound can be written as ‹y› or ‹igh›.

lie	time	my	high
tried	shine	shy	right
cries	drive	try	flight

Read the words in the stars and draw pictures for them in the moons.

tie

pie

fly

sky

bike

kite

light

night

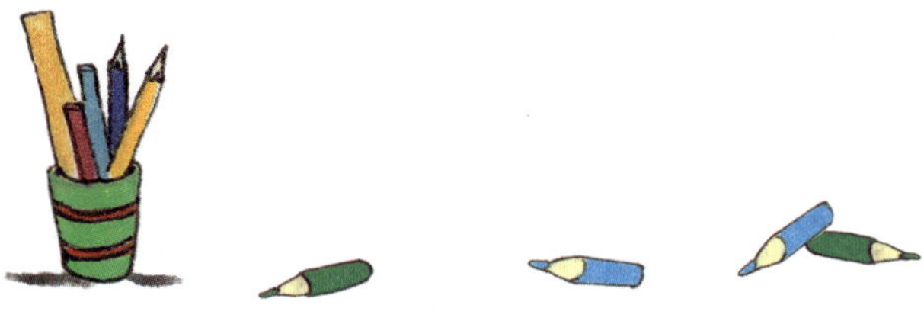

Handwriting

Practice writing these letters. Remember to start at the top and go down. Then come straight back up and over.

r r r r r r

n n n n n n

m m m m m

h h h h h h

Write the capital letter next to each lower-case letter.

n N

o ___

p ___

r ___

q ___

s ___

t ___

v ___

u ___

w ___

x ___

z ___

y ___

Look Find the tricky bit.	**Copy** then **Cover**	**Write** then **Check**	**Have another go!**
live	live		
give	give		

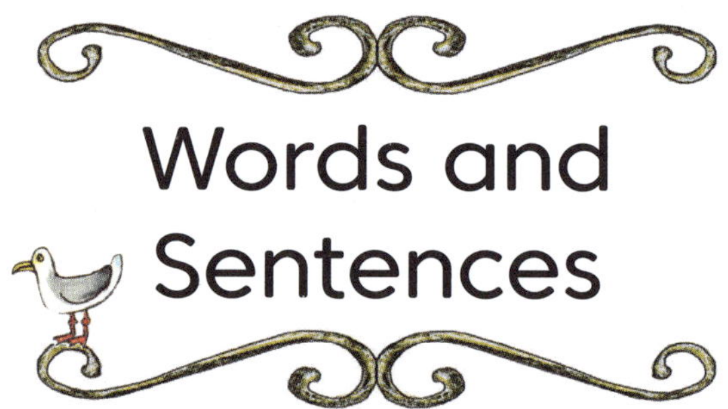

Step 2
Unit 10

Both the /oa/ and /ou/ sounds can also be written as ‹ow›.

coat toad
oak soap

grow borrow
yellow slow

shout south
mouse flour

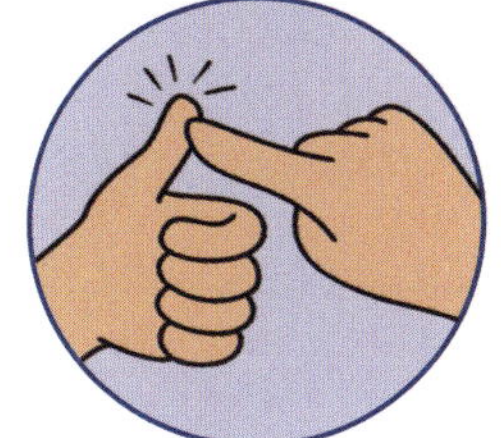

town brown
growl flower

Read the words below and draw a picture for each one.

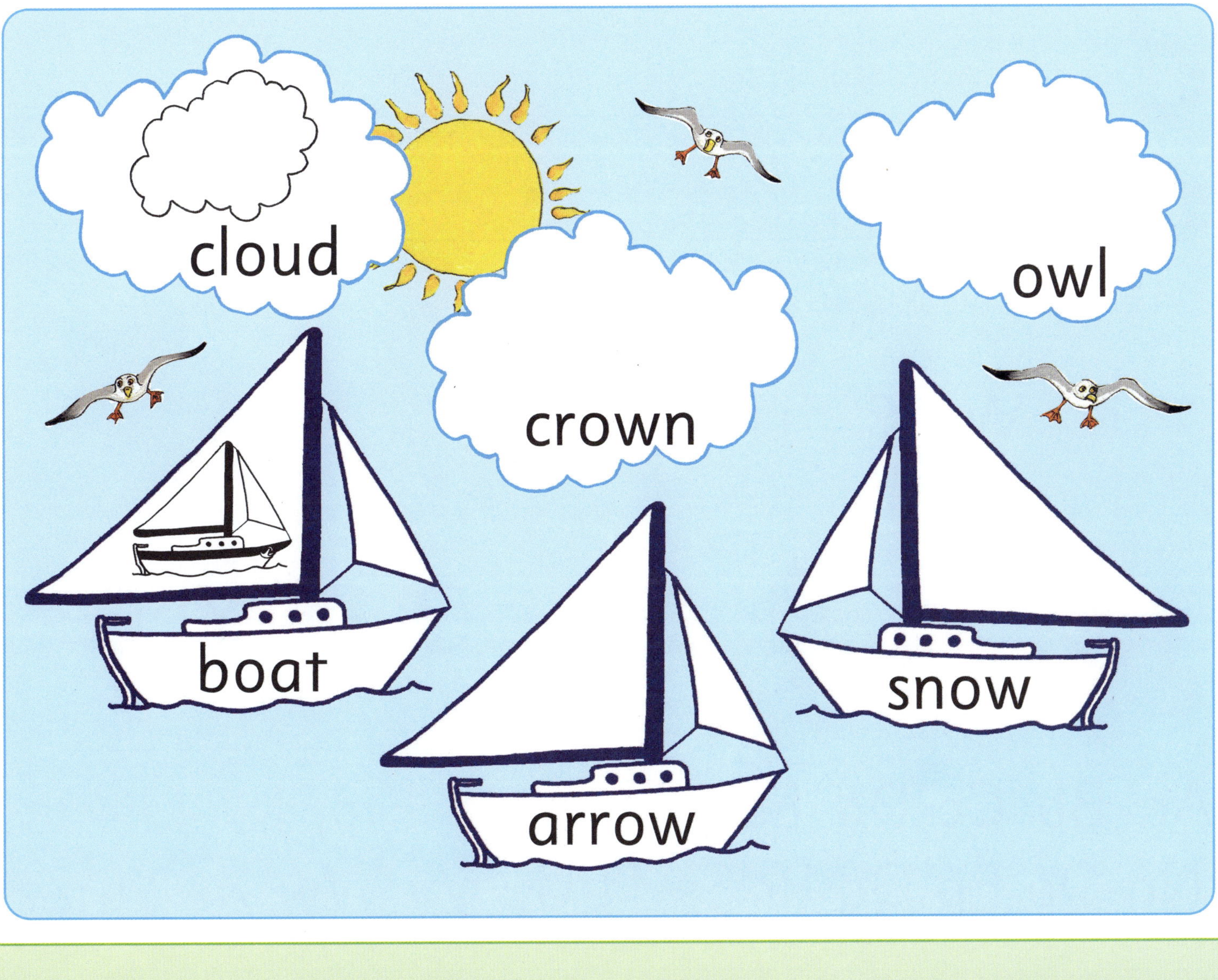

cloud

owl

crown

boat

snow

arrow

Handwriting

Practice writing these caterpillar /c/ letters.

c c c c c c

a a a a a a

d d d d d d

o o o o o o

g g g g g g

q q q q q q

Put these letters into alphabetical order.

k w e n

___ ___ ___ ___

Q D Y G

___ ___ ___ ___

Aa Bb Cc Dd Ee Ff Gg Hh Ii Jj Kk Ll Mm

Nn Oo Pp Qq Rr Ss Tt Uu Vv Ww Xx Yy Zz

Look Find the tricky bit.	**Copy** then **Cover**	**Write** then **Check**	**Have another go!**
little	little		
down	down		

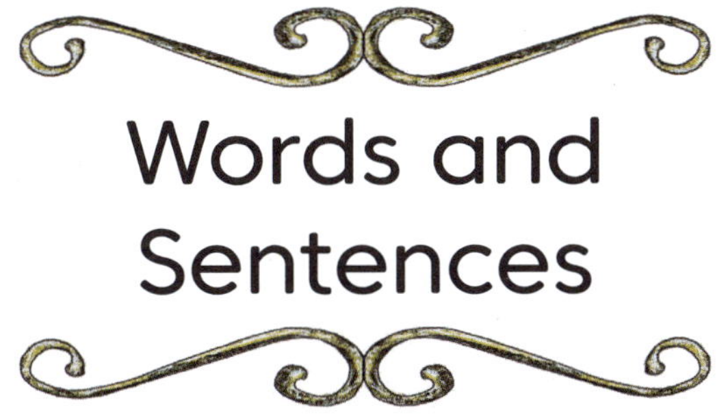

Step 2

Unit 11

ir and ur as /er/

As well as ‹er›, the /er/ sound can be written as ‹ir› or ‹ur›.

ladder girl burn hammer first

burger purple bird church

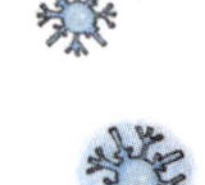

Read the words below and draw a picture for each one.

summer

winter

skirt

shirt

nurse

purse

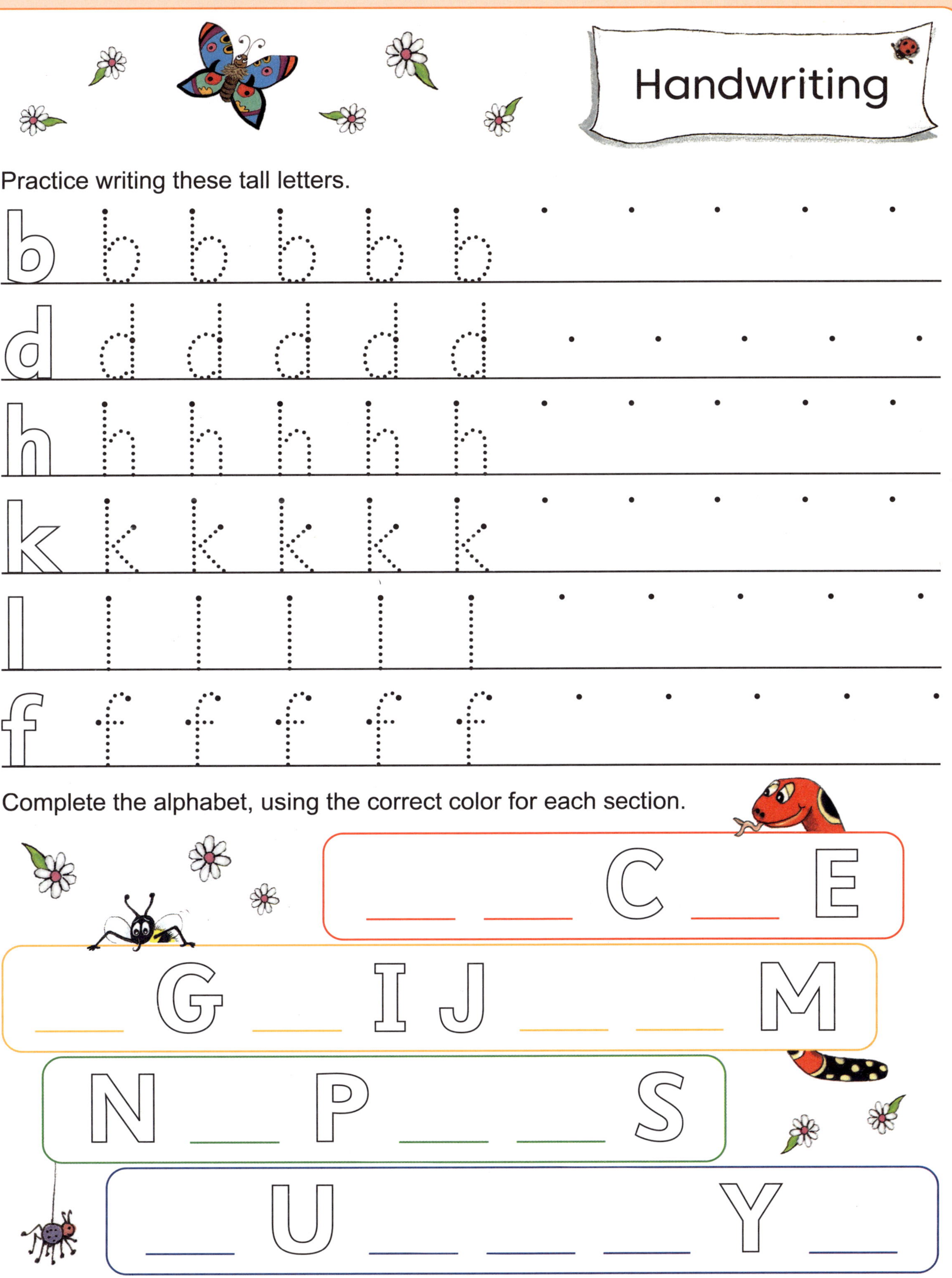

Handwriting

Practice writing these tall letters.

b b b b b b

d d d d d d

h h h h h h

k k k k k k

l l l l l l

f f f f f f

Complete the alphabet, using the correct color for each section.

___ ___ C ___ E

___ G ___ I J ___ ___ M

N ___ P ___ ___ S

___ U ___ ___ ___ Y ___

Look Find the tricky bit.	Copy then Cover	Write then Check	Have another go!
what	what		
when	when		

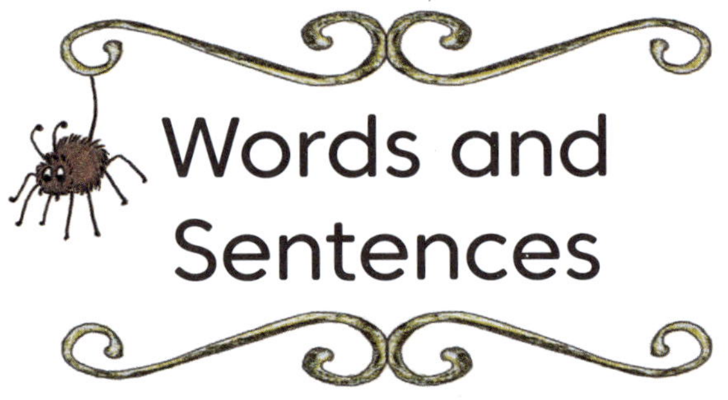

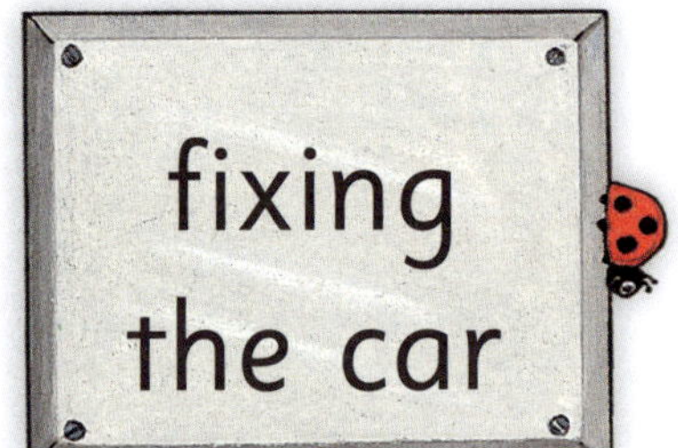

Step 2
Unit 12

As well as ‹ue› and ‹u_e›, the /ue/ sound can be written as ‹ew›.

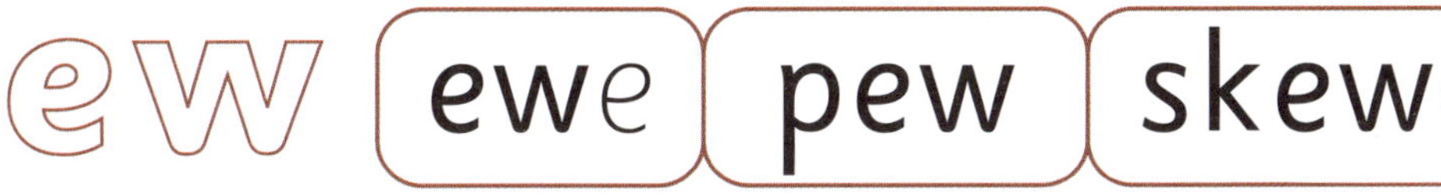

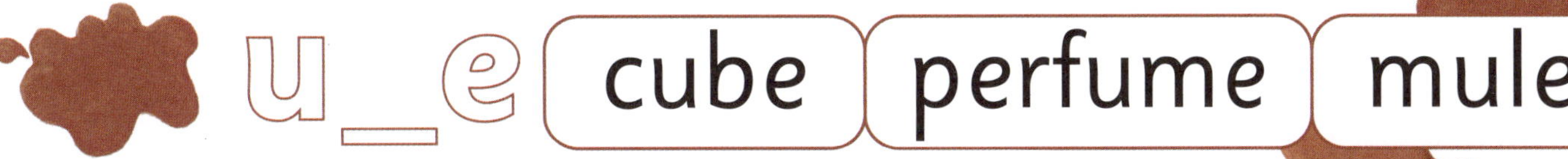

Read the words at the top of the page and write the correct word under each picture.

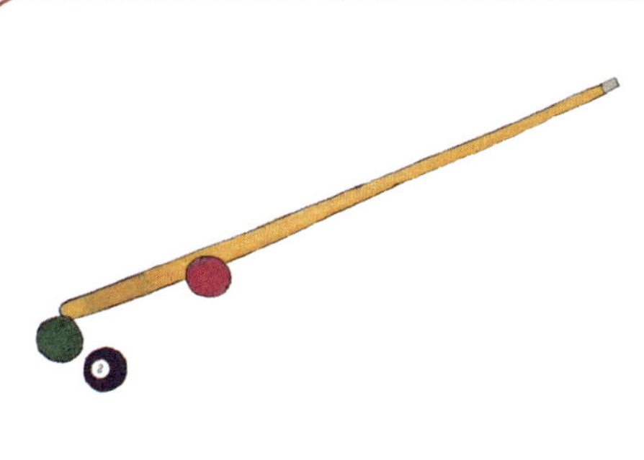

Handwriting

Practice writing these letters, which have tails that go under the line.

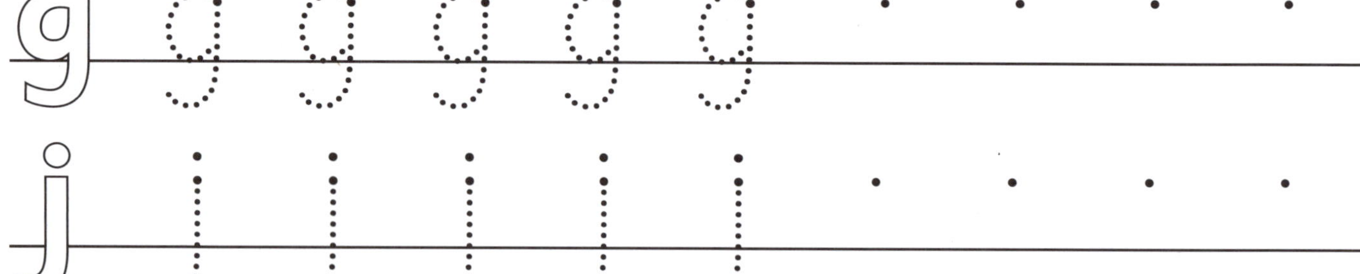

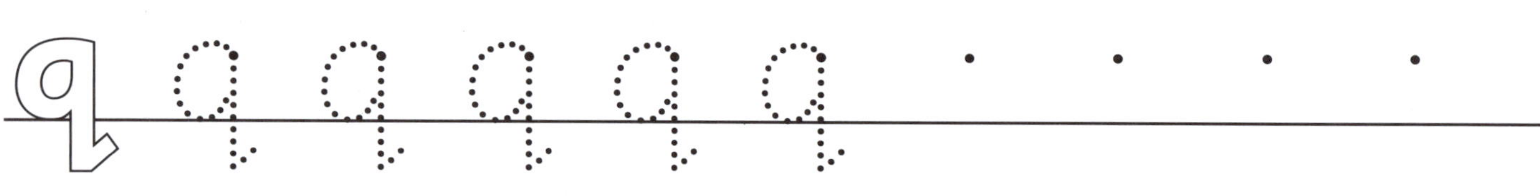

Complete the alphabet, using the correct color for each section.

Look Find the tricky bit.	Copy then Cover	Write then Check	Have another go!
why	why		
where	where		

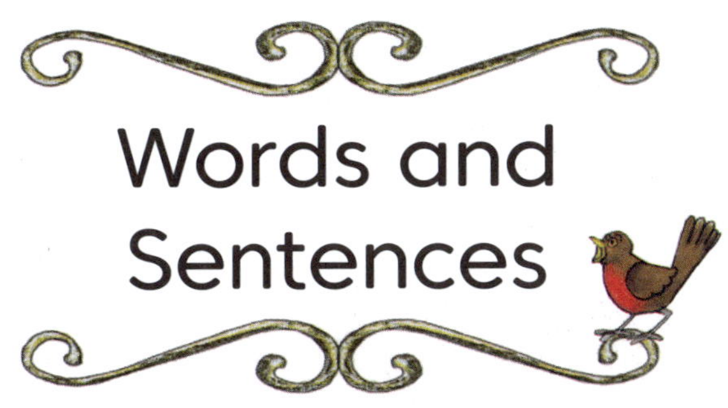

Step 2

Unit 13

aw
au
al

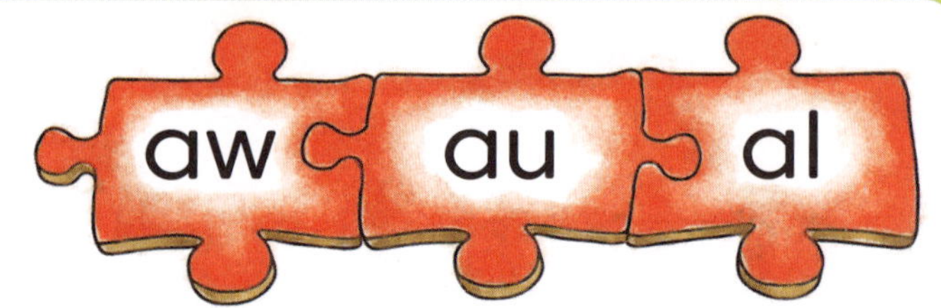

The /o/ sound can also be written as ‹aw›, ‹au›, or ‹al›. Match the words and pictures in the jigsaw pieces. Then color the pictures.

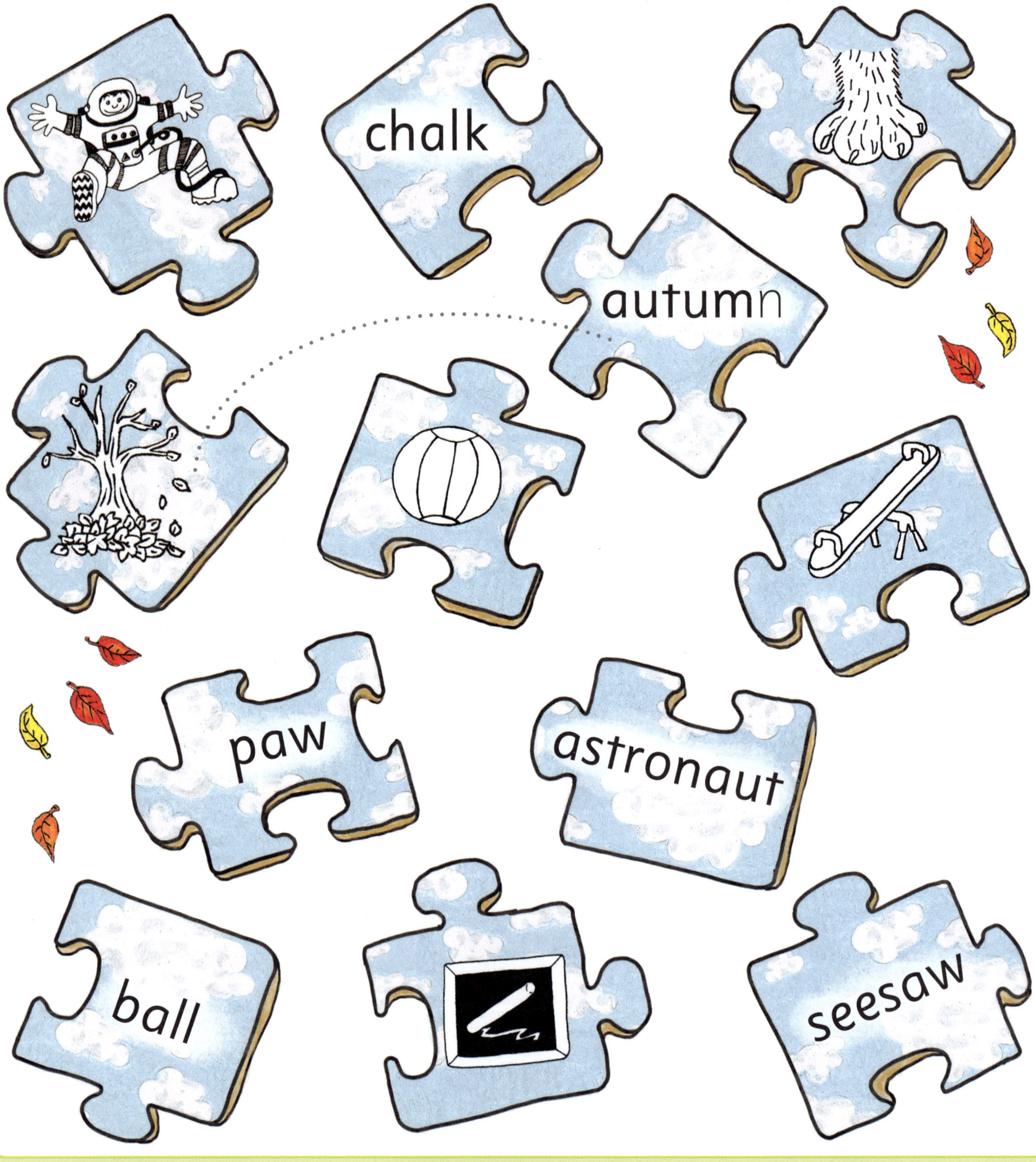
chalk
autumn
paw
astronaut
ball
seesaw

Handwriting

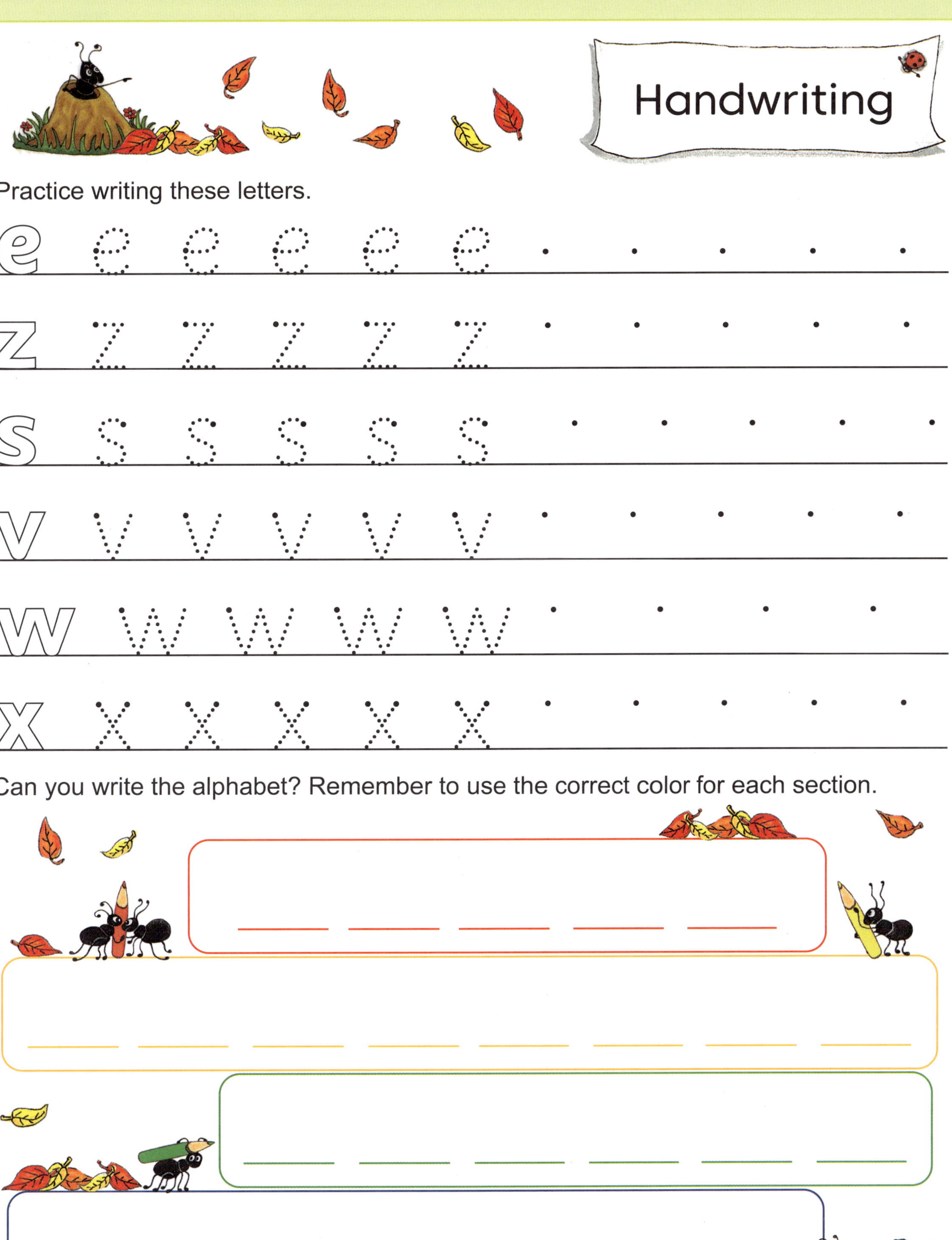

Practice writing these letters.

Can you write the alphabet? Remember to use the correct color for each section.

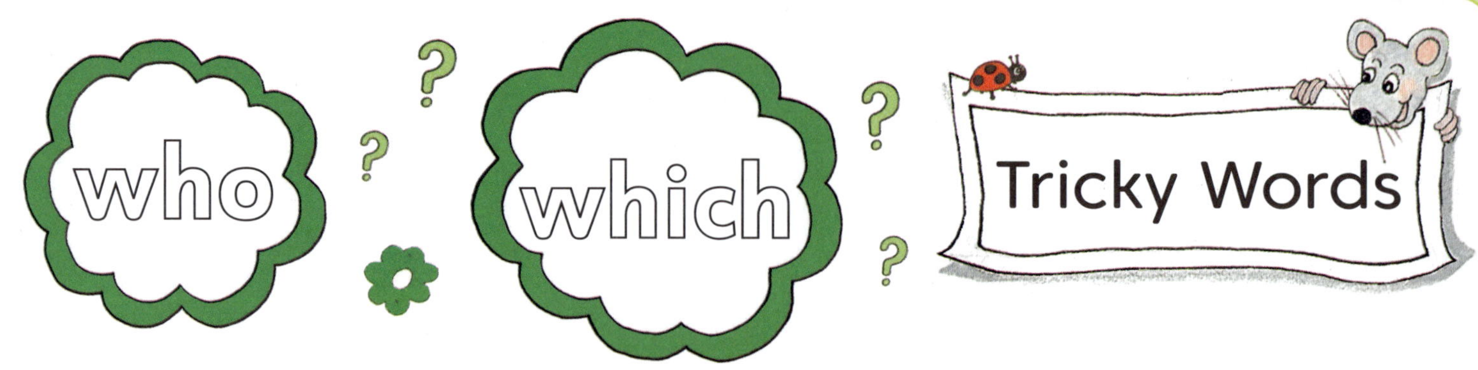

Look Find the tricky bit.	Copy then Cover	Write then Check	Have another go!
who	who		
which	which		

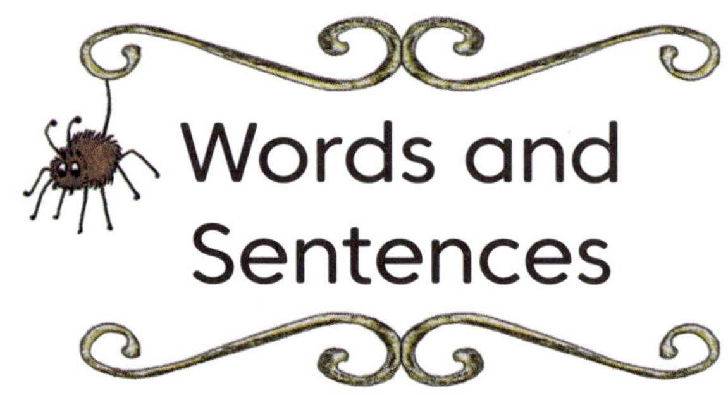

Tricky Words

Step 2 Unit 8 Read the tricky words. Can you find them hidden below?

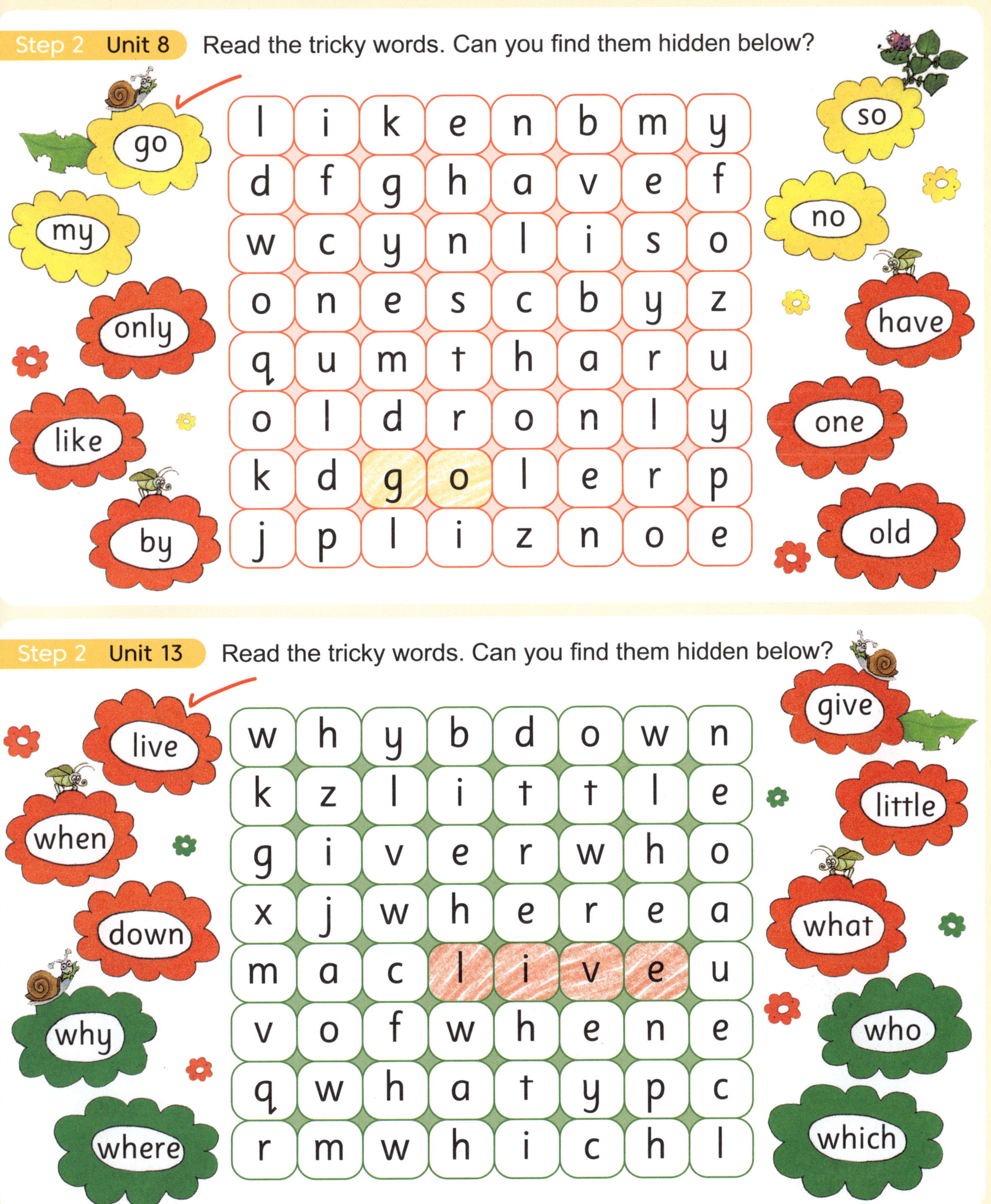

Step 2 Unit 13 Read the tricky words. Can you find them hidden below?

Alternatives

Step 2 Unit 7 Animal anagrams: put the letters in the right order.

n s ai l

___ ___ ___ ___

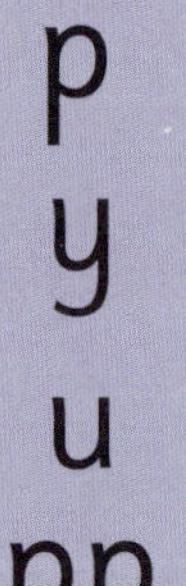

p y u pp

___ ___ ___ ___

k n s a_e

___ ___ ___ ___ ___

Step 2 Unit 8

l s ea

___ ___ ___

ck i ch

___ ___ ___

k ar sh

___ ___ ___

Step 2 Unit 9

u d ck

___ ___ ___

l y f

___ ___ ___

ee p sh

___ ___ ___

Step 2 Unit 10

r ow c

___ ___ ___

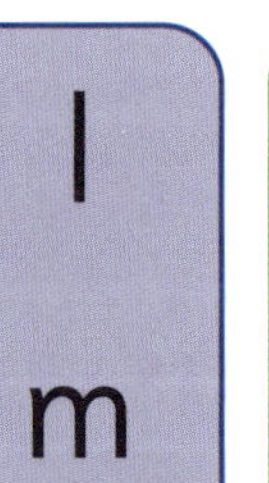

l m o_e

___ ___ ___ ___

g t oa

___ ___ ___

Alternatives

Step 2 Unit 11 Animal anagrams: put the letters in the right order.

ir d b

_ _ _

ow c

_ _

o er tt

_ _ _

Step 2 Unit 12

l ow

_ _

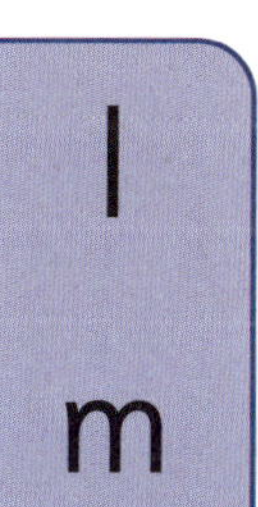

l m u_e

_ _ _ _

k a y

_ _ _

Step 2 Unit 13

k h aw

_ _ _

c ea p ck o

_ _ _ _ _ _

t k or s

_ _ _ _ _

Well done!

You have completed Step 2

Welcome to Step 3

Step 3
Unit 1

ph as /f/

In some words, the /f/ sound is written as ‹ph›.

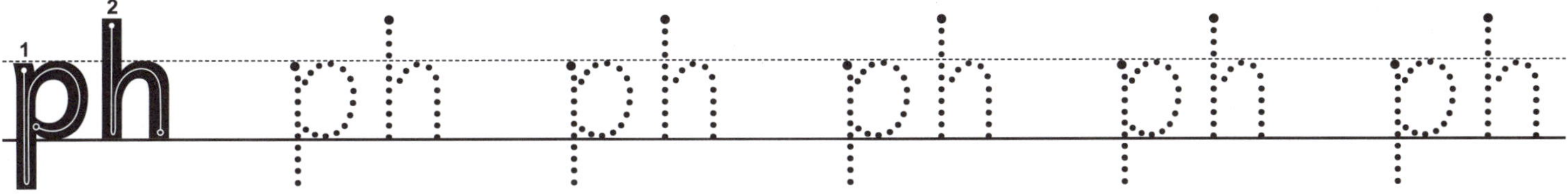

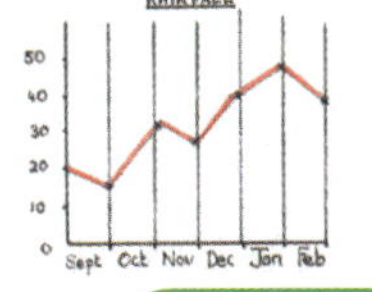

photo nephew graph

alphabet saxophone orphan

pamphlet sphinx

Read the words below and draw a picture for each one.

elephant

dolphin

phone

phantom

Write over the dotted letters and add the missing letters.

any a_y _ny an_ _n_

many m_ny _a_y man_

Finish these sentences by adding either *any* or *many*.

Have you got ______ milk?

How ______ ducks are on the pond?

Listen and write.

____

____

Read the tricky words and color the flowers using either red or green.

Words and Sentences

Read the list of things you might find out at sea and add them to the picture.

1. a boat
2. six fish
3. a big crab
4. a starfish
5. a flying seagull
6. three red shells
7. a man in the boat
8. a shark with big teeth
9. a yellow sun in the sky

Step 3

Unit 2

Soft c

When the letter ‹c› is followed by ‹e›, ‹i›, or ‹y›, it usually makes a /s/ sound.

race city fancy mice bouncy

prince acid cycling voice accident

Read each word below and write it under the matching circus tent. Color the pictures.

ice cream

rice
circle
face
cycle
fence
pencil
ice cream
circus tent

Write over the dotted letters and add the missing letters.

more m_re _or_ mo_e

before be_or_ _ _fo_e

Finish these sentences by adding either *more* or *before*.

I went swimming ________ lunch.

"We need ______ butter," said Dad.

Listen and write.

____

____

Read the tricky words and color the flowers using a green pen or pencil.

Words and Sentences

Is it true? Write **yes** or **no** underneath each statement.

The cat is sleeping.

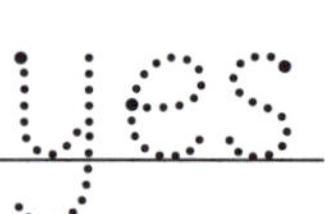

Rabbits are good at hopping.

There are five red socks.

It is three o'clock.

The dragon has ten eggs.

The magpie has a hat.

Step 3
Unit 3

Soft g

When the letter ‹g› is followed by ‹e›, ‹i›, or ‹y›, it usually makes a /j/ sound. Read the words and write each one in the vegetable with the same spelling pattern.

germ margin large dingy engine
allergy ginger magic page energy

Read the words and draw pictures for them.

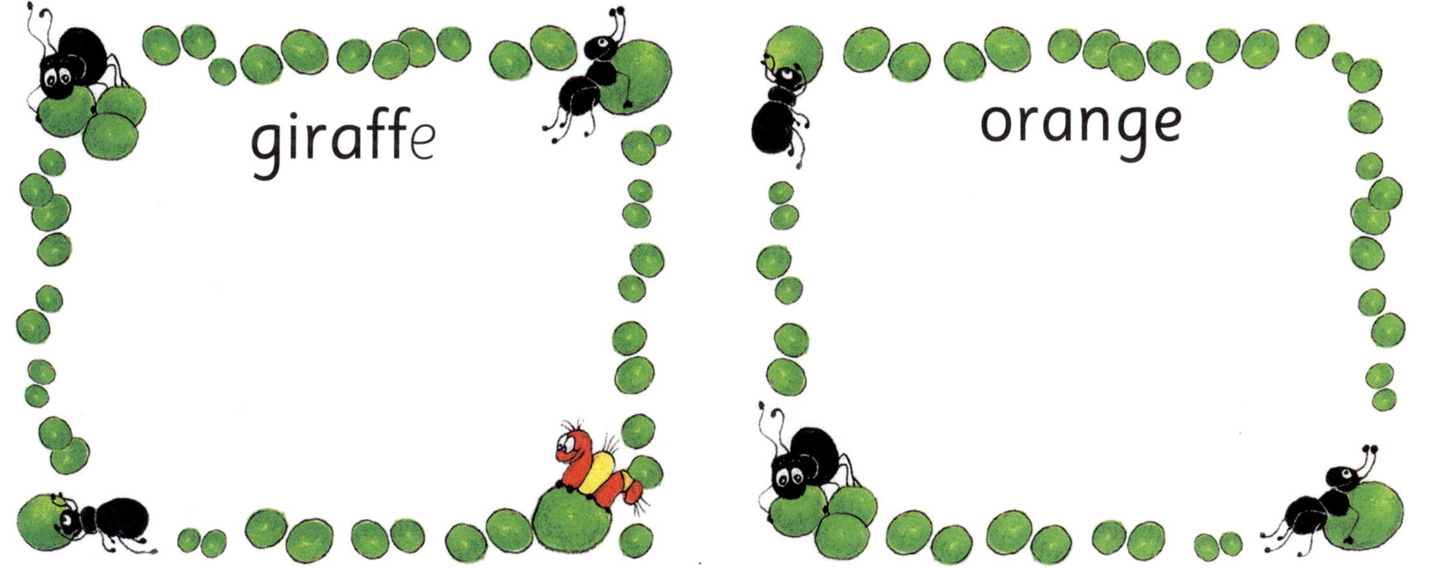

Write over the dotted letters and add the missing letters.

other o__ __er __ther __th__ __

were wer__ __e__e w__ __e

Finish these sentences by adding either *other* or *were*.

We ________ skipping in the park.

Jim has lost the __________ sock.

Listen and write.

____

____

Read the tricky words and color the flowers using a green pen or pencil.

Words and Sentences

What is happening at the park? Choose the right word to complete each sentence.

1. The dog is carrying a ________. stone | stick
2. There is a cat in the ________. tree | boat
3. The fox is looking at the ________. cat | rabbit
4. The ducks ________ on the pond. quack | quit
5. The children have a bat and ________. ball | wall
6. The bird in the tree is ________. singing | swinging

Step 3

Unit 4

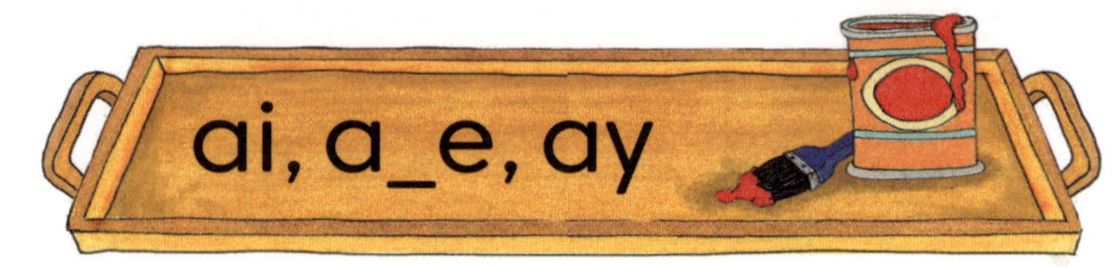

There are three main ways to write the /ai/ sound. Read the words below and then write them in the correct /ai/ spelling.

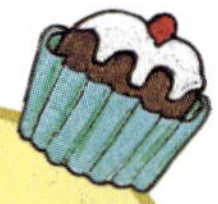

a_e

whale

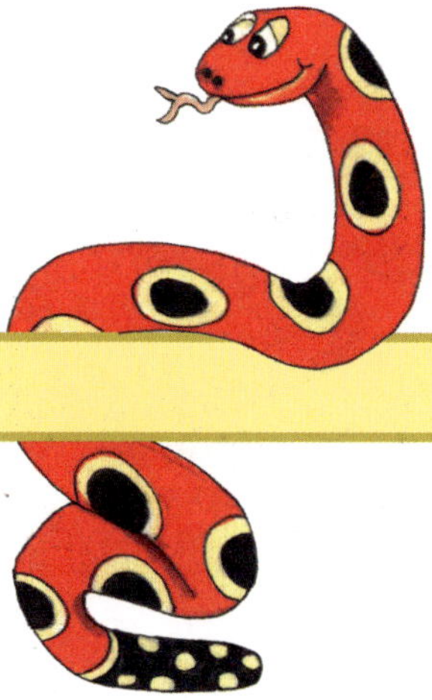

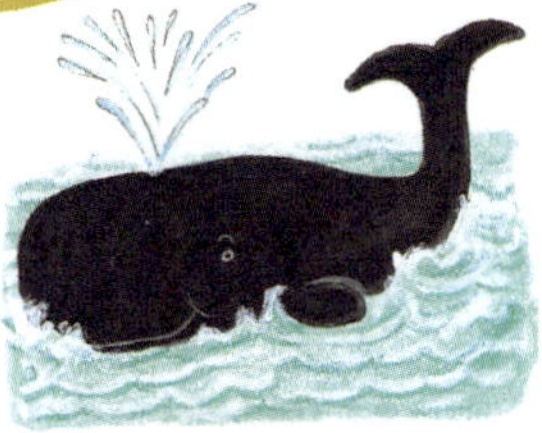

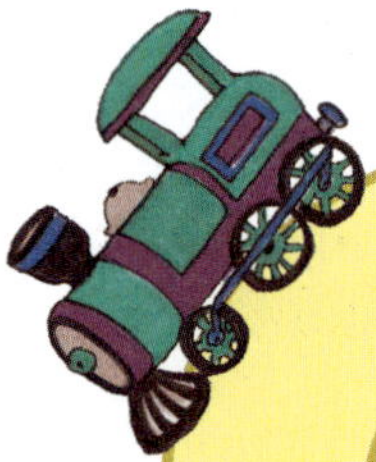

ay

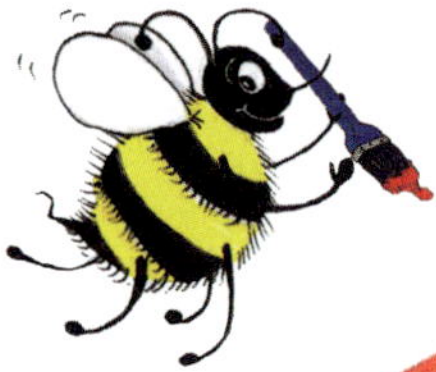

ai

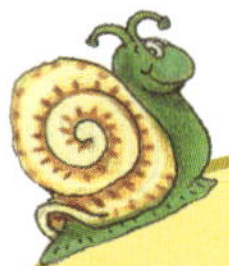

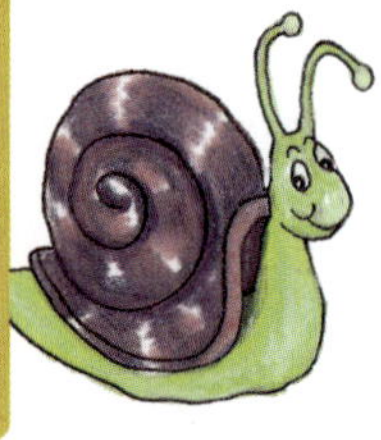

whale
paint
play
snake
train
tray
name

may cake
tail
snail hay

Write over the dotted letters and add the missing letters.

because b_c__s_ _e__u_e

want w_nt _a_t w_n_

Finish these sentences by adding either *because* or *want*.

Do you ________ to help?

He went home __________ he felt sick.

Listen and write.

____

____

Write inside the outline letters to spell the tricky word *because*.

big elephants Catch ants Under Small elephants.

Read each sentence and find the matching picture.

The sun is hot.

I sleep in a bed.

The boat is sailing.

The soap is on the dish.

This sock is long.

He is running.

Step 3
Unit 5

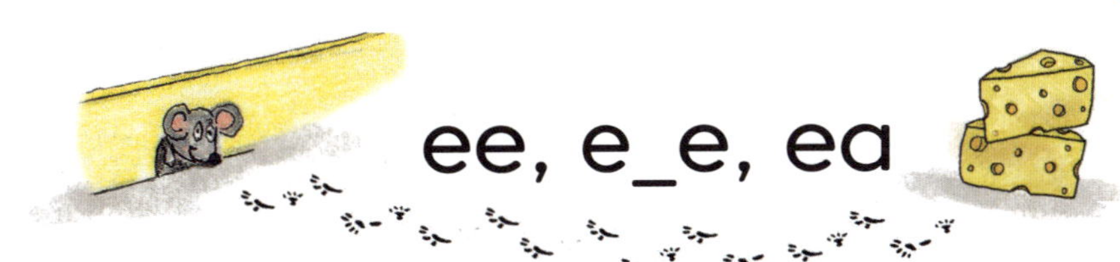

ee, e_e, ea

As well as ‹y› at the end of a word, there are three main ways to write the /ee/ sound.

speed sneeze toffee three

evening complete extreme trapeze

teacher peanut peach teapot

Read the words below and write them in the correct /ee/ spelling.

tea
bee
these
athlete

ee: bee

ea

eve
seal
read
teeth

feet
beak
sleep
theme

e_e

Write over the dotted letters and add the missing letters.

saw s__ _a_ __w

put p_t _u_ p__

Finish these sentences by adding either *saw* or *put*.

I ______ my drum back in the toy box. 

Yesterday, we ______ Dad do a handstand.

Listen and write.

____

____

Read the tricky words and color the flowers using a green pen or pencil.

Words and Sentences

Read the phrases and draw a picture for each one.

a rabbit in a hutch

a bat in a tree

a black cat in red boots

three snails in the rain

the moon and some stars

a big rainbow in the sky

Step 3
Unit 6

There are four main ways to write the /ie/ sound. Read the words below and then write them in the correct /ie/ spelling.

light
fly
like
pie
night
prize

igh: light

y

ie

lie
time
right
high
reply

i_e

my die
kite
sky tie

Write over the dotted letters and add the missing letters.

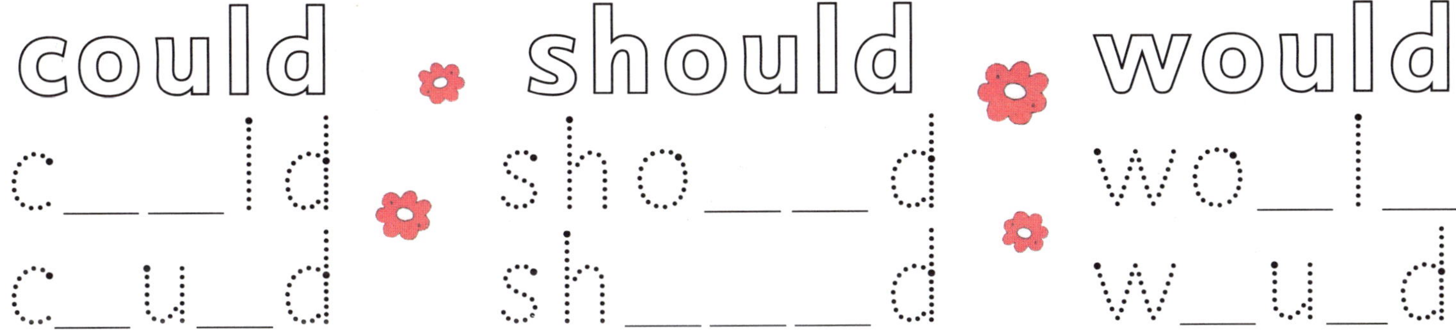

Finish these sentences by adding *could*, *should*, or *would*.

________ you like some more tea?

I ________ put the tent up now, if you like.

We ________ clean out the hamster's cage.

Listen and write.

Read the tricky words and color the flowers using either green or pink.

Words and Sentences

Match the two sentences that describe each picture.

I can see a hen.	He likes to hop.
The oak tree is tall.	He has big horns.
The goat is running.	It has a brown shell.
A frog is in the pond.	They have a bucket.
A snail sits in the rain.	Its leaves are green.
The boys play in the sea.	Her beak is yellow.

Step 3
Unit 7

oa, o_e, ow

There are three main ways to write the /oa/ sound.

coach float coast raincoat

tadpole home stone joke

rainbow elbow shadow window

Read the words below and write them in the correct /oa/ spelling.

those
toast
throw
goat
slow
bone
blow

rose
oak
snow
nose
loaf

Write over the dotted letters and add the missing letters.

Finish these sentences by adding *right*, *two*, or *four*.

He got all his sums ________.

Two plus two is ________.

The ________ boys are twins.

Listen and write.

____

____

____

Read the tricky words and color the flowers using either green or pink.

Words and Sentences

Read the sentences and fill in the gaps. Color the pictures to match.

The tall oak ______ is green.

My _____ is long. It has red and black stripes.

My brown ______ has a big collar.

The little green ______ jumped into the pond.

The ______ shines in the night.

I found a _______ in the garden. It had a yellow shell on its back.

Step 3

Unit 8

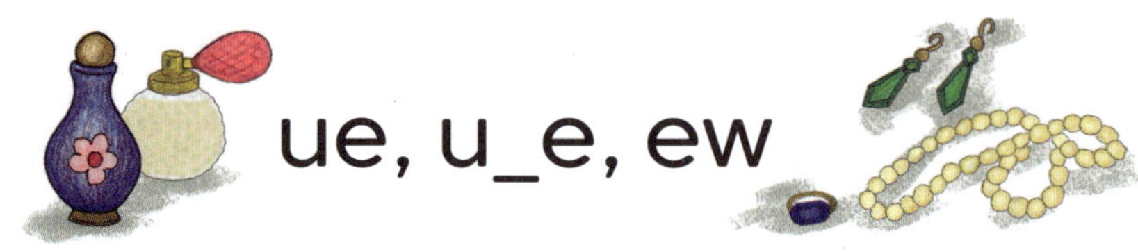

ue, u_e, ew

Read these words. If the /ue/ sound does not work, try the /oo/ sound.

bluebell argue untrue barbecue

ruler use excuse rude

fewer unscrew threw nephew

Read the words below and write them in the correct /ue/ or /oo/ spelling.

u_e: cube

few
glue
cube
statue

blue
June
chew
rescue

ue

ew

pew
cute
flute
jewel

Write over the dotted letters and add the missing letters.

Finish these sentences by adding *goes* or *does*.

He ________ to the park with his sister.

When ________ the match start?

Listen and write.

____

____

Read the tricky words and color the flowers using a pink pen or pencil.

Words and Sentences

Look at the animals in the zoo and then answer these questions.

1. How many monkeys are in the tree? ____________
2. Which animal has a trunk? ____________
3. What is the tall bird called? ____________
4. Where is the crocodile swimming? ____________
5. Who has black and white stripes? ____________
6. How many giraffes are there? ____________

Make as many words as you can from the letters in the word:

elephants

sleep

____

____

____

____

____

____

____

Step 3
Unit 9

There are two main ways to write the /ou/ sound.

loud	about
count	ground
sound	flour

flower	crowd
downhill	growl
shower	vowel

Read the words below and write them in the correct /ou/ spelling.

owl
mouse
brown
mouth

ou: mouse

cow
found
cloud
clown

ow

Write over the dotted letters and add the missing letters.

made m_d_ _a_e m___

their th__r __ei_ th___

Finish these sentences by adding *made* or *their*.

We _______ some cakes yesterday.

They played with _______ dog.

Listen and write.

Read the tricky words and color the flowers using a pink pen or pencil.

Words and Sentences

Write a story about a party and draw a picture for each part. Begin by completing the sentences below and then add your own ideas.

We had a party for ________

We ate some ________

Step 3
Unit 10

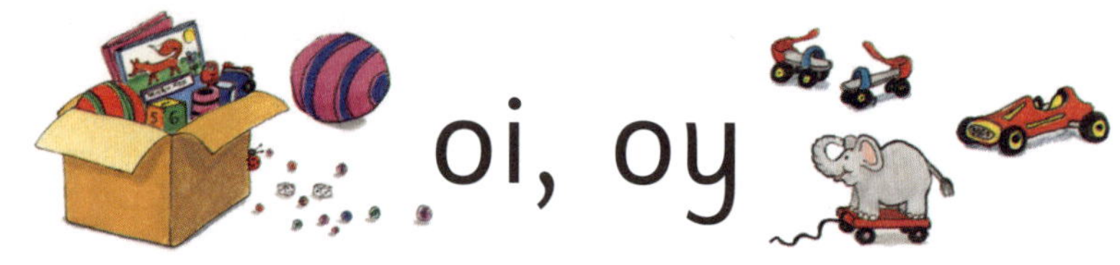

oi, oy

There are two main ways to write the /oi/ sound.

oi	oy
boil join	royal oyster
tinfoil oilcan	destroy employ
ointment coil	annoy loyal

Read the words below and write them in the correct /oi/ spelling.

joy
coin
boy
spoil

coil
toy
point
enjoy

Write over the dotted letters and add the missing letters.

Fill in the gaps by adding *once*, *upon*, or *always*, and then finish the story.

________ ________ a time, there was 

a little house in a big wood. The wood was

________ dark... ________________________

Read the tricky words and color the flowers using a pink pen or pencil.

Words and Sentences

Complete the story of Moat Farm, using the words below.

lives	Neb	Ben	Farm	sheep
Green	sheepdogs		hill	truck

1

This is Moat Farm.

2

Farmer Green ________ on Moat Farm.

3

Ben and Neb are ____________.

4

______ and ______ help on the farm.

5

This morning, Ben and Neb run up the ______...

6

...and help round up the ________.

7

Farmer ________ checks that the sheep are well.

8

Neb and Ben rest in the back of the ________.

Step 3

Unit 11

er, ir, ur

There are three main ways to write the /er/ sound.

butter	helicopter	river	number
third	birthday	twirl	thirsty
purple	Thursday	curl	Saturday

Read the words below and write them in the correct /er/ spelling.

dinner
shirt
purse
letter

er

dinner
____
____
____

ir

____
____
____
____

bird
fur
sister
girl

hurt
diver
first
turn

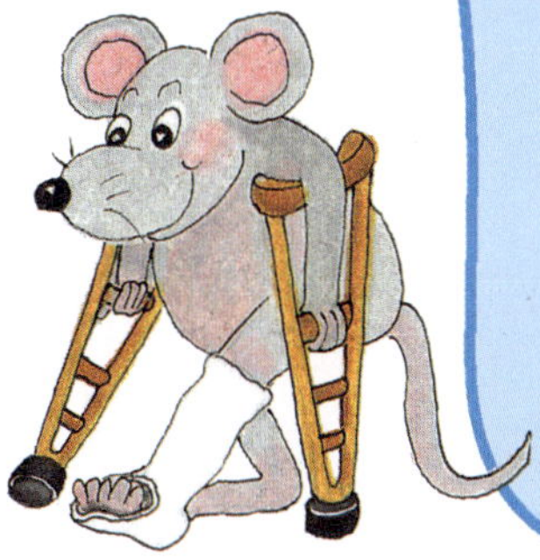

ur

____
____
____
____

also of

Tricky Words

eight

Write over the dotted letters and add the missing letters.

also of eight

_ _ s _   o _   _ _ _ _ t

_ _ _ o   _ _   _ i _ h _

Finish these sentences by adding *also*, *of*, or *eight*.

There are lots ______ sheep on the farm.

I ______ saw some cows in the barn.

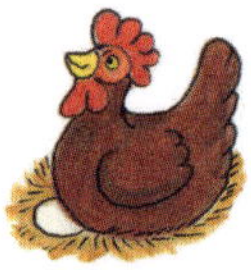

I counted ______ chickens in the yard, too.

Listen and write.

____

____

____

Read the tricky words and color the flowers using either pink or brown.

Words and Sentences

Read the clues and write the answers in the crossword grid.

1. This will help you to find your way.
2. If you are sick, you go to see the ____.
3. This small insect lives in a nest underground.
4. If you go camping, you may sleep in this.
5. You wash with ____ and water.
6. This animal hisses.
7. The time of year when it is cold.
8. A chick hatches from this.
9. This is on the end of your arm.
10. This is a very big stone.
11. The sky is blue and the trees are ____.
12. At night it is ____.

Step 3

Unit 12

There are three main alternative spellings for the /o/ sound.

yawn strawberry shawl drawing

laundry August astronaut autumn

snowball chalk beanstalk taller

Read the words below and write them in the correct /o/ spelling.

saw
haunt
ball
pause

aw

saw
____
____
____

walk
small
hawk
launch

au

____
____
____
____

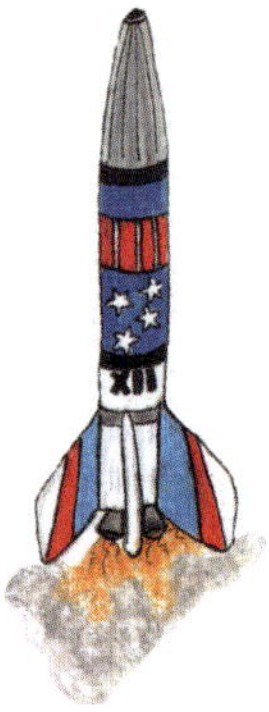

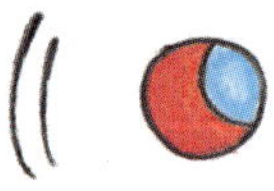

wall
cause
draw
crawl

al

____
____
____
____

Write over the dotted letters and add the missing letters.

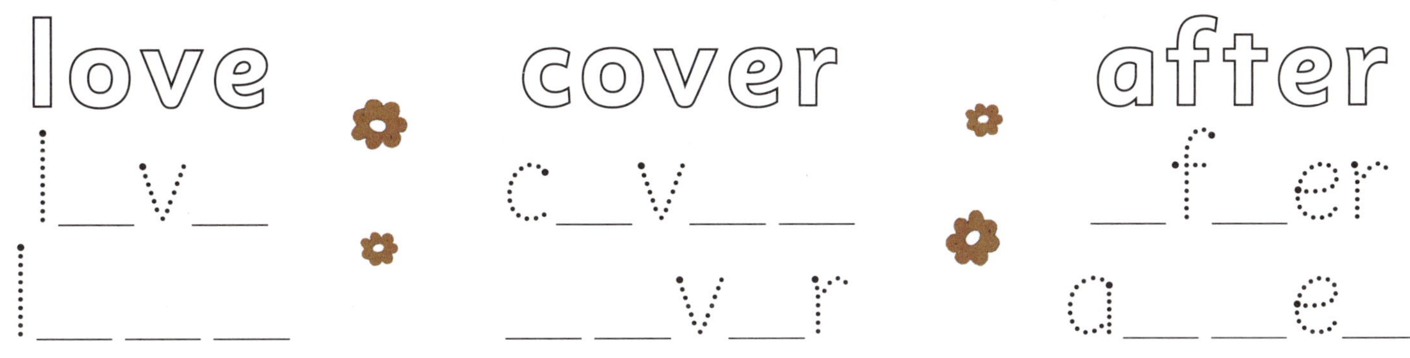

Finish these sentences by adding *love*, *cover*, or *after*.

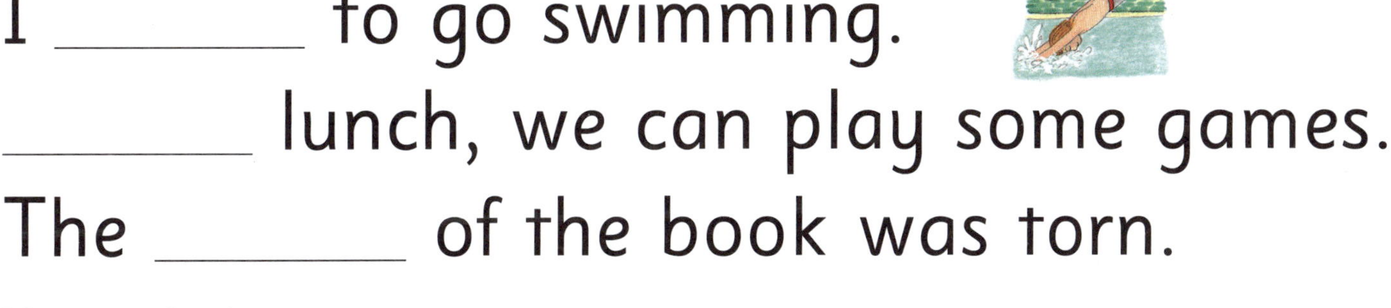

Listen and write.

____

____

____

Read the tricky words and color the flowers using a brown pen or pencil.

Words and Sentences

What is happening on the beach? Look carefully and answer the questions below.

1. What are the children doing on the rocks?

____

2. What can you see in the tide pool?

____

3. What is on the top of the sandcastle?

____

4. How many legs does an octopus have?

____

5. How many beach umbrellas are there?

____

6. What sort of animal is a seagull?

____

Step 3
Unit 13

air, ear, are

The /air/ sound can be written ‹air›, ‹ear›, or ‹are›.

air air hair chair pair

ear bear wear tear pear

are stare rare square dare

Read the words inside the salmon and join them to the right bear. Color the pictures.

hare
fairy
bear
pear
scarecrow
stairs

Write over the dotted letters and add the missing letters.

every mother father

_ v _ _ y m _ th _ _ f _ th _ _

ev _ _ _ m _ _ _ _ _ f _ _ _ _ _

Finish these sentences by adding *every*, *mother*, or *father*.

My ______ and ______ are my parents.

I go dancing ______ week.

Listen and write.

Read the tricky words and color the flowers using a brown pen or pencil.

Words and Sentences

Read the story of the midnight feast and answer the questions below.

Once upon a time, there was a king called Alfred. His wife was Queen Matilda. They lived in a castle with a cat called Fluffy.

One night, King Alfred was hungry. So he got up and made himself some cheese sandwiches to eat. Some crumbs from the sandwich fell onto the floor.

A mouse saw the crumbs from her mouse hole in the corner of the room. She could have a midnight feast if she was quick and quiet. She crept out and had just reached the crumbs when Fluffy woke up. The mouse ran for her hole as quickly as she could. Fluffy ran for the mouse as quickly as he could. The mouse reached her hole. She was hungry, but safe!

1. What is the king's name? ____________________
2. What is the queen's name? ____________________
3. What sort of animal is Fluffy? ____________________
4. What did King Alfred make to eat? ____________________
5. Who saw the crumbs on the floor? ____________________
6. Who saw the mouse? ____________________
7. Did the cat catch the mouse? ____________________

Read, Write, and Review

Step 3 Units 1 to 6 Write inside each lower-case letter and write the capital letter next to it.

A a ___ b ___ c ___ d ___ e

___ f ___ g ___ h ___ i

___ j ___ k ___ l ___ m

___ n ___ o ___ p ___ q ___ r ___ s

___ t ___ u ___ v ___ w

___ x ___ y ___ z

Step 3 Unit 13 Put these letters into alphabetical order.

R j E o N z i U

___ ___ ___ ___ ___ ___ ___ ___

t L a D

___ ___ ___ ___

Read, Write, and Review

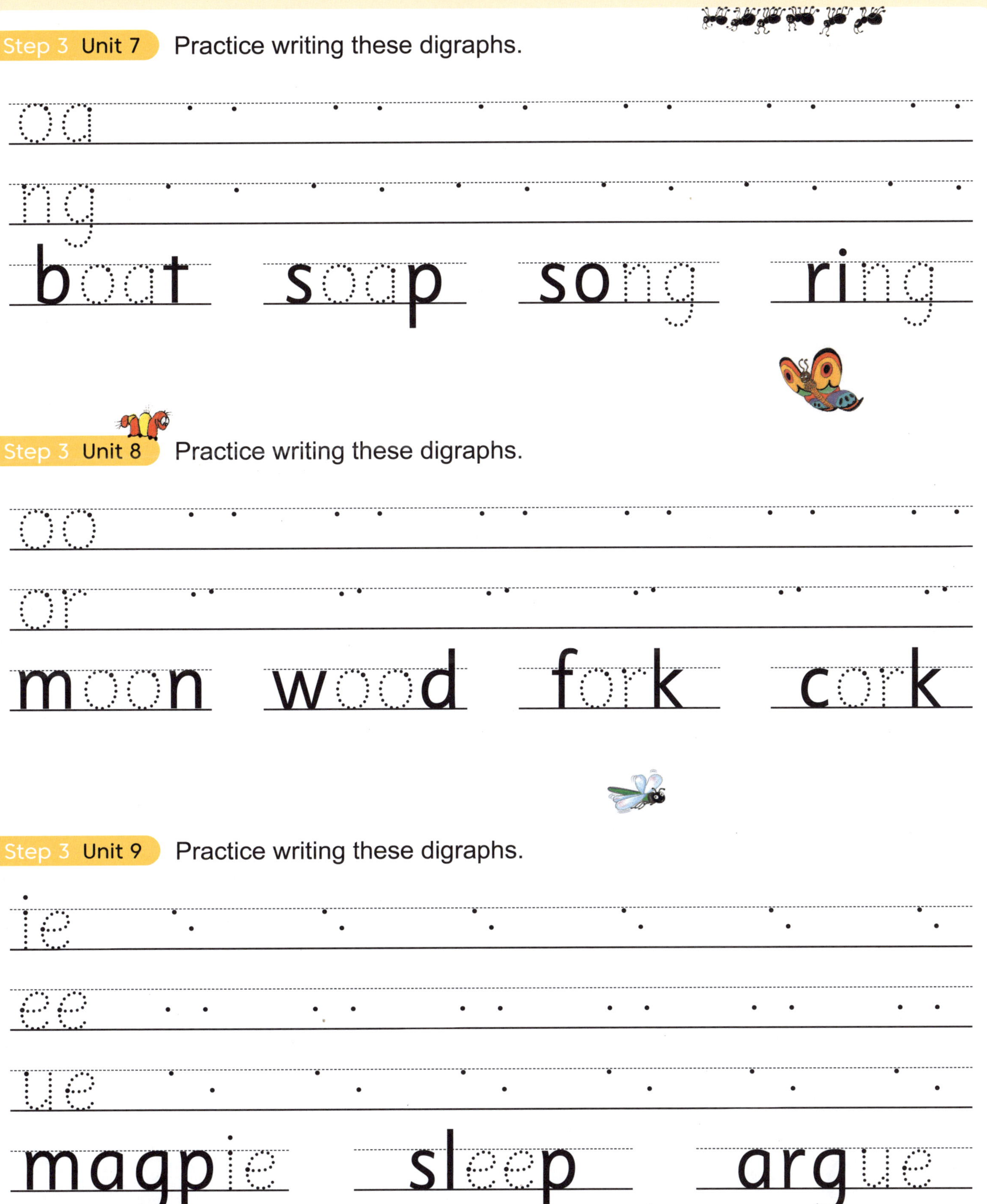

Step 3 Unit 7 Practice writing these digraphs.

oa

ng

boat soap song ring

Step 3 Unit 8 Practice writing these digraphs.

oo

or

moon wood fork cork

Step 3 Unit 9 Practice writing these digraphs.

ie

ee

ue

magpie sleep argue

Read, Write, and Review

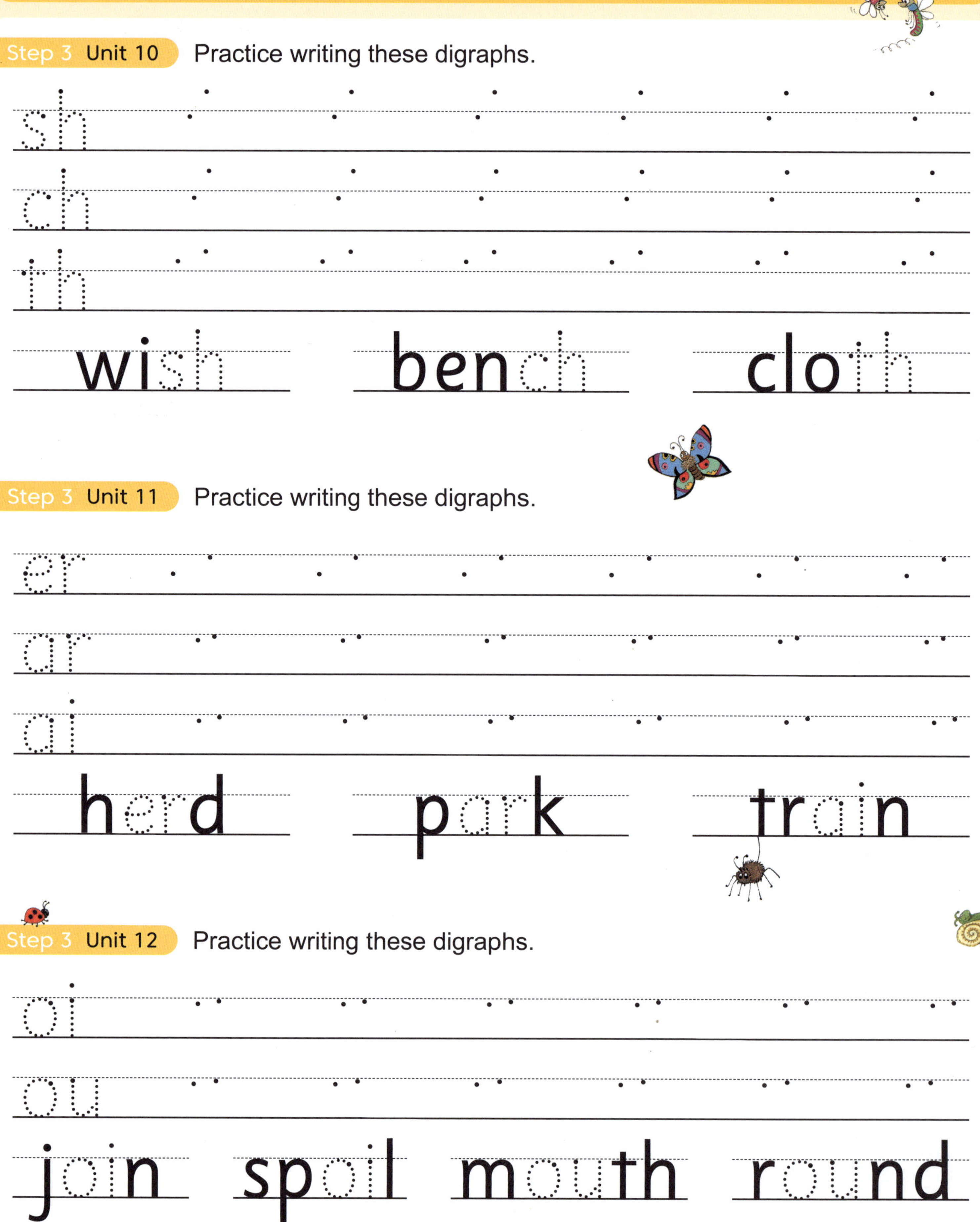

Step 3 Unit 10 Practice writing these digraphs.

sh

ch

th

wish bench cloth

Step 3 Unit 11 Practice writing these digraphs.

er

ar

ai

herd park train

Step 3 Unit 12 Practice writing these digraphs.

oi

ou

join spoil mouth round

Tricky Words

Step 3 Unit 5 Write over the dotted words in the tricky word flowers. Then find them in the wordsearch.

Tricky Words

Step 3 Unit 9 Write over the dotted words in the tricky word flowers. Then find them in the wordsearch.

b	w	o	l	k	a	j	e	i	n
q	u	i	w	o	u	l	d	a	p
z	m	a	d	e	n	g	o	e	s
o	v	u	t	h	e	i	r	n	y
s	c	o	u	l	d	e	x	q	u
g	l	y	c	a	r	i	g	h	t
d	o	e	s	b	o	t	w	o	r
j	e	f	o	u	r	s	h	a	p
v	i	n	g	s	h	o	u	l	d
o	r	t	h	a	k	y	e	z	i

Tricky Words

Step 3 Unit 13

Write over the dotted words in the tricky word flowers.
Then find them in the wordsearch.

every once also cover

eight upon mother after

of father love always

e	q	u	p	l	o	v	e	s	k
d	c	o	m	f	a	t	h	e	r
o	k	r	e	v	e	r	y	i	g
j	o	f	b	e	i	g	h	t	l
q	u	a	l	w	a	y	s	k	o
s	c	o	v	e	r	l	y	a	b
d	z	a	m	o	t	h	e	r	y
a	f	t	e	r	g	u	p	o	n
z	i	c	h	a	l	s	o	x	e
i	b	r	o	n	c	e	r	y	m

Alternatives

Step 3 Units 1 to 13 Practice saying the short and long vowel sounds.

Read each pair of words. Decide which word matches the picture and write it underneath.

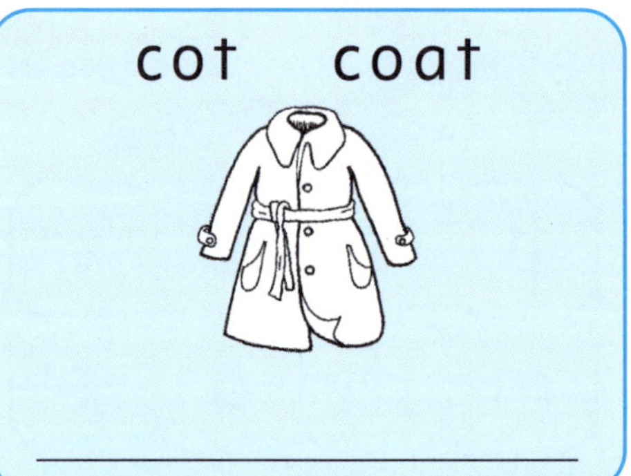

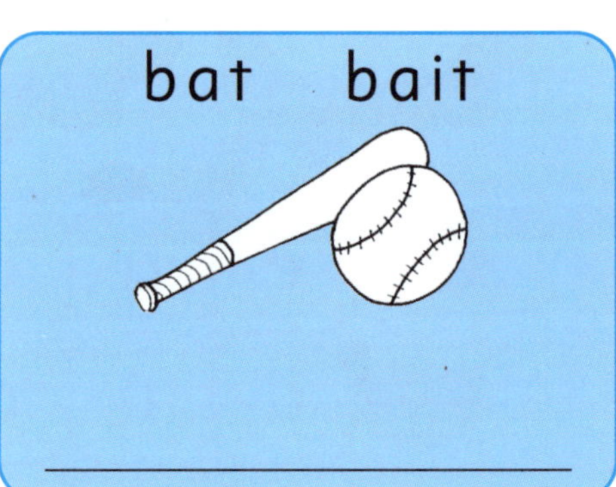

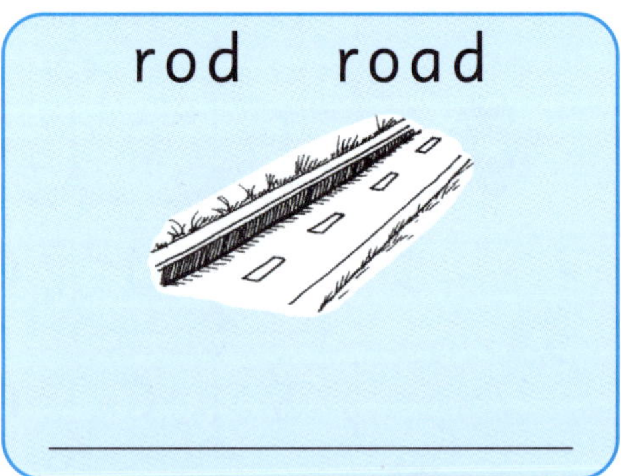

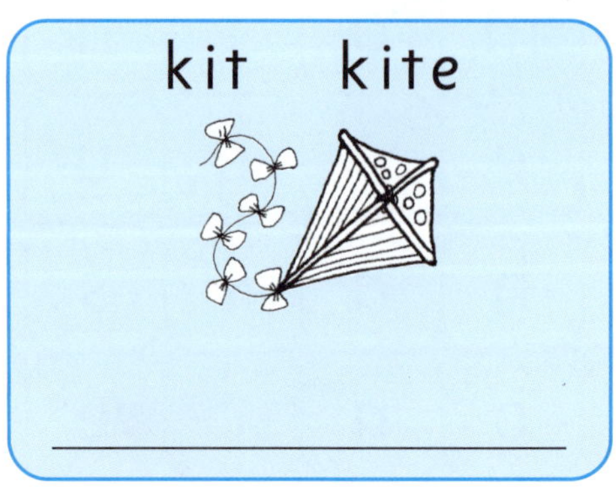